Why We Fall

How Not to Sabotage Your Career —
Your Relationships — Your Life!

DOROTHY BURTON

ISBN: 978-0-9776087-3-7

Cover by Marion Designs, Stockbridge, Georgia
Author photograph by Cecilia Bolar
Hair by Irish of WOW! "IF LOOKS COULD KILL"
HAIR STUDIO, Dallas, Texas

Text Design: Lisa Simpson
www.SimpsonProductions.net

A publication of Dorothy Burton, LLC

Printed in the United States of America

To those who never saw it coming — the fall.
And, to those who are one bad decision away
from losing it all.

Looking back, my life so far seems like one long obstacle race, with me as its chief obstacle.

- Jack Parr

Contents

FOREWORD

Arrogance, greed, pride, infidelity. Many have lost careers, relationships and reputations because of them. From the pulpit to the classroom, from city halls to the halls of Congress, and from corporate America to small-town America; there has never been a time in modern history where every aspect of our culture has been so distressed and the resulting emotional, financial, and spiritual carnage so wretched.

Using solid biblical principles so simple even high school students can understand, Dorothy Burton explores the seven principal reasons behind the often-surprising downfall of those esteemed as being honest, disciplined, respectable, intelligent and committed to God, family, community, and career. "Good" people whom no one would ever suspect would steal from the treasury they have been entrusted to oversee, have a sordid affair, take money under the table, be fired from their job or use their position of influence to exploit others.

Written from a biblical frame of reference, nearly every page is filled with wisdom and encouragement as Dorothy helps the reader identify, control, and overcome things common to us all, but often missed or carelessly dismissed when we insist upon living our life our way apart from God.

While others are often the blame for many of our problems, some things we bring upon ourselves. This book will help you avoid becoming your own worst enemy as you learn how not to sabotage your career, your relationships — your life.

DR. TONY EVANS
Author, Speaker
President, The Urban Alternative
Senior Pastor, Oak Cliff Bible Fellowship,
Dallas, Texas

ACKNOWLEDGMENTS

... to my husband Michael, you have been my strength, my sounding board and my encourager. I am the woman I am today because of you.

... to our beautiful daughter Jessica, you are truly a gift.

... to my Pastor, Dr. Tony Evans for helping me understand God really does cause all things to work together for good. Thank you for your wise and life-saving counsel.

... to Cathryn Nathan — the Prayer Warrior. Thank you for your prayers and wisdom.

... to Keith Saunders for your beautiful cover design.

... to my sisters, Laretha Miles and Elois Huckaby for always being there for me; and to my brothers, Arthur Miles, Jr., and Thomas Steward (Bubba) — I love you both.

INTRODUCTION

Have you ever done something so incredibly stupid and so out of character that looking back, there are no words, plausible excuses or rational reasons why you did what you did — yet at the time, it made all the sense in the world to do it? I have. For me, it cost me a job. For you it may have cost you the same, perhaps your marriage, or an opportunity to be a mom because of a botched abortion years ago that now impacts your ability to have children. Or, a lost opportunity to be a dad because you were afraid of commitment and responsibility. Today that same son or daughter you shunned has turned out to be one any parent would be proud to call their own; however, they now want nothing to do with you.

With time and maturity, and looking back through the 20/20 lens of hindsight, many of us if we could, would undo some things we did; and, make different and wiser decisions than we made. But life rarely affords "do-overs."

It doesn't matter how religious, smart, successful, beautiful, popular, wealthy, famous, seeming-to-have-it-all together we are, the fact is, we all make mistakes, use poor judgment and spew offensive words we can never take back.

I have bookshelves brimming with books on how to be a leader, how to have a successful career, how to be a woman of God, how to... you name it, and I probably have it. Yet, as a born-again, Bible believing, successful, married-to-a-doctor, with a big house in the suburbs (complete with pool and spa), committed woman of faith, I still failed — and failed miserably.

This book has its genesis in an obscure article I wrote several years ago for the Texas Municipal League magazine, "Texas Town & City." The article entitled, "Why We Fail — Avoiding the Evils of Elective and Appointed Office" was written as an instructional tool for those who serve in the fishbowl of the public arena. I had grown tired of learning about, reading about and seeing up close and personal, the astonishing number of public leaders committing career suicide. Some were friends, others just colleagues — but most were good, solid people who because of bad choices experienced spectacular downfalls.

The article turned out to be more popular than I could have ever imagined and was published in numerous publications which jump-started a career in writing and speaking that I in no way planned. I discovered that people, not just those in high profile elected positions, but others as well, from executives to church secretaries had experienced painful falls from grace. However, because of their status or position within their communities found the pain, shame, and guilt of their failure unbearable. Many had given serious thought to ending it all. I empathized with them and could understand the depth of their pain. I too had walked in their shoes. I thank God for my pastor, Dr. Tony Evans, and my husband Michael, who literally prevented me from blowing my brains out because I too had been in a pit so deep that I didn't want to live anymore.

Life is tough and tougher still for those who have messed up, given up, and who see no way back up. However, I have found that as tough as life can sometimes be, God is tougher. He is tough enough to carry us through the toughest life storms and tough enough to help us overcome our toughest challenges. You *can* get back up again.

I struggled for weeks on just this Introduction alone because I did not want to be as transparent as the Lord was leading me to be. However, over time, I realized the world is in desperate need of transparency from authentic people who have been where they are and who aren't afraid or ashamed to reach out by saying, "I messed up too, and this is what worked for me."

This book is not for the faint of heart and may at times hit you squarely between the eyes as it at times did me. But Rome is burning and my heart weeps for those who through mistakes and careless choices are losing careers, reputations; and moreover, the simple joy of living. Life is not meant to be this way. We don't know what we don't know; but, what we don't know about ourselves can damage us in ways that can sometimes be permanent or take years to remedy.

Why We Fall is a reflection of us all. What began as a personal journey of self-discovery and recovery, led me to understand that the ties that bind us and the ambitions that can blind us are rooted in our common weaknesses; not in our uncommon strengths. It is what I call our commonality of imperfection. Conventional wisdom puts it this way — none of us is perfect and we all make mistakes. Godly wisdom however, brings it home, "Indeed, there is not a righteous man on earth who *continually* does good and who never sins" (Eccl. 7:20).

Take heart. That person or persons looking down their sanctimonious nose on you because of your failures are likely drowning in a silent sea of their own. Those who relish in wiping your face in the dirt of your past often do so in order to shine the light on yours in order to keep others from digging into theirs. So calm down, take a deep breath, and understand that we all fall. My hope is that after reading this book, you will gain a better perspective on why you may have done what you did that precipitated your fall, or better still, cause you to tread more lightly on what you will learn is shaky ground. We all at some juncture in our life's journey will fail. We are all in the same boat.

I am not a psychologist, psychiatrist, counselor, televangelist, preacher or pastor. This is my first book and mine is not a household name. Yet my name isn't important. What is important is that I am a shipmate on the boat with you; one who has fallen overboard many times, shipwrecked, and at times nearly drowned. Though slippery at times, I nonetheless found my footing and so can you.

An African proverb reads, "He who learns, teaches." My prayer is that you will learn as I have learned that it is not always external enemies that can hurt us most, but the ones we carry on the inside.

The greatest tragedy when it's time to die is to realize we never took the time to discover why we lived.

– Dorothy Burton

I wanted to live my life my way,

never mind what God had to say.

I didn't have time to stop and ask,

"God, what should I do, what is my task?"

I had a great career and was a huge success,

until He called me to take my rest.

Then I learned from God the King,

I had spent my life doing the wrong thing!

CHAPTER 1

⤳

Forfeiting Our Purpose: Running the Wrong Way

"Before I formed you in the womb I knew you, And before you were born I consecrated you..."

Jeremiah 1:5

It was New Year's Day, 1929. The Rose Bowl in Pasadena, California was teeming with rowdy fans in giddy anticipation of what promised to be a Rose Bowl showdown between two defensive powerhouses: the home team California Golden Bears and the boys from down south, the Georgia Tech Yellow Jackets.

This would be a day for the record books — not because of the astonishing number of points that would be scored nor for the electrifying runs of an elusive star running back; but for a spectacularly stunning fumble return by Golden Bears center, Roy Riegels.

Minutes into a scoreless second quarter, Tech halfback Jack "Stumpy" Thomason was hit and fumbled the ball. Both teams scrambled wildly for the loose ball as it bounced freely up field. Bears center Roy Riegels scooped the ball from the air. He took off toward the Georgia Tech goal line with teammates and defenders in hot pursuit. He was only 30 yards away from hitting pay dirt when he was shoved into a would-be tackler.

With a move seen typically in limber speedsters and not lumbering centers, Roy pivoted to get free and as he spun around, he completely lost his bearings. Thinking he was still heading in the right direction and unencumbered, he ran hard and fast toward the end zone that loomed ahead. Unaware he had done a complete spin around, Roy had no way of knowing the end zone ahead was not his opponent's, but his own.

With the roar of the crowd reverberating in his ears, the flow of adrenaline pumping through his veins, and perhaps visions of grandeur dancing in his head, he charged ahead toward the goal line — unaware he was heading in the wrong direction. Roy's teammate and quarterback, Benny Lom chased him down while screaming, "Stop Roy, you're going the wrong way!" By the time Lom caught up with Roy at the ten-yard line, Roy had run over 60 yards in the wrong direction. Lom grabbed him and slowed him only to have Roy shake him off and selfishly growl, "Get away from me, this is my touchdown!"

Realizing what was at stake, Lom with dogged determination again caught up with and grabbed Roy just as he reached the three-yard line. Roy finally realized something had to be terribly wrong. By then however, it was too late as Georgia Tech players who no doubt couldn't believe their unexpected but welcomed gift, swarmed him at the one-yard line. This proved to be the play that would cost the Golden Bears the Rose Bowl victory. Rather than risk a turnover and a possible go-ahead score by Georgia Tech, the Bears decided to punt from their end zone. The punt was blocked for a safety. That gave Tech a two-point advantage that turned out to be the difference in the final score as Georgia Tech went on to win the historic game eight to seven.

Roy, though he enjoyed a full life, never shook the label or the ridicule as Roy "Wrong Way" Riegels — a name that stuck with him until he passed away decades later at the age of 84.[1]

Roy's story has become a favorite among many for a number of reasons. I believe it is one of the greatest illustrations of how a random, seemingly innocuous encounter can cause one to lose their bearings not just in a game, but in life. Like Roy, if we consistently ignore the shouts of those in our life who see us going the wrong way, we will spend our life running hard and fast in the wrong direction only to discover at the end of our life that we had run the wrong way.

Is This It?

While there has been a whole purpose-seeking movement over the past few years, in counseling people from various backgrounds, I have learned that many of us still don't have a clue as to why we are here and what on earth we are supposed to be doing with our lives.

A plethora of books has hit the market and as baby boomers reach our 50's and 60's, we eagerly seek answers and direction in a world that increasingly doesn't make sense. If the truth were told, a number of us secretly harbor the gnawing doubt that we have not accomplished with any degree of satisfaction that which we set out to eagerly, if not naively, accomplish when we began this journey so many years ago.

Moreover, if we are supposed to be as "there" as we'd like others to believe, why do we feel as though we are still getting there, with the nagging notion and subtle fear that we may die before ever getting there — and leave the planet having never known why we were here?

As we survey the totality of our lives and look back on wrecked marriages, shattered dreams, lost opportunities, disappointing failures, betrayals, bad decisions, dead-end jobs and dead-end relationships — the raw reality of our lives tells us that we, somewhere along the way, have missed the boat.

The two questions and one statement I hear most from others and have even asked and repeated to myself are:

- Where do I go from here?

- Is this all life has to offer?

- This is not the way I wanted my life to end up.

Even more sobering is the realization that time has become a fleeting friend. Where has all the time gone?

More of us are increasingly becoming outcasts from the companies to which we have been so loyal. Our jobs which we mistakenly thought were secure are being outsourced to companies outside of the USA.

For many of us, our new bosses are flip-flop wearing whiz kids young enough to be our grandchildren; but not nearly as respectful. They can text fifteen messages in five minutes, yet can't string together five coherent sentences and treat those as lepers who can. When did having common sense become a liability?

For others of us, our nests are empty, our 401(k)s are evaporating and we look at our aging parents and see our future and it scares the living daylight out of us. Growing old was never an option. Yet with each passing day, it takes more time to get up from the chair and as we look into the mirror, we discover a wrinkle that wasn't there last week; less hair growing on the top of our head and more hair sprouting in odd places where we didn't even realize there were hair follicles.

Still more of us can't escape the sinking feeling that our best days are behind us as we have spent our time spinning our wheels and all we have to show for it is stuff that no longer satisfies, with the growing suspicion that in our haste to make it, we have missed it. We can't figure out exactly what the "it" is that we have missed, but whatever "it" is, we grow more certain with each passing day that without notice, "it" has quietly passed us by.

Too many of us in our drive to capture the elusive brass ring, forsook our families and neglected our relationships as we hastened to earn the respect of people who no longer matter and to earn degrees that are now dust catchers. We sought to prove our worth by working hard to make an impression on our bosses, while failing to make time for our children. Now in the silence of our lonely existence we long for the noise of the distant past when our children romped noisily through now empty rooms and we regret time lost and time hurried because there was always somewhere to go and someone to meet.

The Thank You cards are barely in the mail and you already regret your choice. You steal glances at your new spouse while he or she isn't looking or stare coldly into the darkness as he or she sleeps. All you now want is out. It wasn't love, but the pressure of passion that brought you to the altar and already the red hot embers have chilled to ice cold blue. The depressing thought of spending the rest of your life with this person is unbearable. You want to run but where can you go since your parents are so proud and everyone at church holds you up as the model couple? The pounding yet hushed evening question is not, "Honey, how was your day?" But, "Lord, what was I thinking?"

The generation who claims that 60 is the new 40 is finding it increasingly difficult to settle down to the serene, mind-numbing boredom of the routine; while Generations X, Y and Z are growing up mostly taking cues for finding their purpose not from God, mom or dad, but from rap videos, athletes and raunchy sitcoms.

Discovering why we were created and what we were created to do will determine the degree of our success and happiness; or, the degree of our failure. This should be priority. Otherwise our decisions and choices will lead to failure after failure; frustration after frustration; and at the end of the day, there will be no sense of satisfaction at all. Even more, when God calls us home we will sadly discover that like Wrong Way Roy, we spent our entire lives running in the wrong direction.

Where We Go Wrong

Quite simply, our purpose is to do that which God designed us to do through the optimal use of our talents and gifts, given to us by Him in order to glorify Him and be a blessing to others. Our purpose is not just for our ease, comfort, prosperity or fame and is never for us alone. It is our assignment, set aside and given to us by God before we were embryos or fetuses. Our purpose is not the same as our job, although it could be. What's more, it comes naturally. When you discover your purpose, you likely will not be able to explain how you do what you do in the way that you do it. Moreover, others will recognize how almost without effort you are able to do it — and do it well. No task will bring you greater joy than flowing in your God-given purpose.

God had our purpose in mind before He had us in mind and created us in the physical to carry out that which He had predetermined in the spiritual. That is why it is foolish and pointless to question why you were born the way you were born, into the family to which you were born, with the features and personality with which you were born because you were born to fulfill a predetermined purpose. God wrapped your flesh around your purpose. That is one reason why you can find no peace or will be continually frustrated in dead-end job after dead-end job; or worse, waste time mimicking someone else's purpose because you are trying to force in the physical before you find out in the spiritual what you are to do. Not that God "needs" any of us, but to more clearly make this point I will use the cliché, "necessity is the mother of invention." God had a need to be met, a mission to be accomplished, or a task to be fulfilled. He knew the specifications, the attributes, the time period and type of personality that would be needed to fulfill that need, mission or task He had in mind. That is where you and I come into play. We have been perfectly outfitted for our purpose but the problem is too many of us walk around in the wrong outfit most of our lives, never bothering to consult God about our wardrobe.

Not only is our purpose predetermined, but it has a time limit. We only have so much time to do that which we were designed to do yet we live as if we have forever to accomplish it. Wake-up call — the clock is ticking. The Psalmist writes, "Your eyes have seen my unformed substance; And in Your book were all written The days that were ordained *for me,* When as yet there was not one of them" (Ps. 139:16).

Our physical attributes, personality, our degree of intelligence, our abilities and capabilities, idiosyncrasies, experiences (good and bad) and temperament, are all perfectly designed to properly fit together to help us complete with excellence, that which has been assigned to us. The Master Craftsman has designed and constructed us to His specifications to carry out His specific will for His glory, for the good of others, and in the process for the good of our household. If we fail to recognize this, we will go about life as Roy went about his run — in the wrong direction.

The greatest mistake we will make in life is never bothering to go back to the One who created us to ask Him what He had in mind when He created us. Doing this, or not doing this will set the tone for the rest of our lives. Additionally, we need to often go back for tune-ups to make sure at every major juncture in our lives we are still on track. Without knowing we will accept the wrong jobs, marry the wrong person, and spend our time and resources on the wrong things.

No one would use a hammer to trim hedges, nor would anyone use hedge trimmers to hammer a nail. One of the reasons so many of us are stuck in jobs that we hate and boxed into responsibilities that drain our bank accounts and suck the wind out of our sails is because we are misplaced hammers and hedge trimmers — performing duties that we weren't optimally designed to perform.

If you dread going to your job today, and have dreaded going to your job everyday for the past umpteen years, that probably is not the job for you. It never was nor will it ever be. All you will end up doing is just enough to get by, making just enough to get by until you have put in enough time to say good-bye. Am I advocating going out and quitting your job? No. What I am saying however, is that there is a job better suited for your gifts, talents and temperament. You are wasting time you can never get back; forfeiting your joy and the sheer satisfaction of knowing you are right where you are supposed to be. Your stress level will decrease, your sense of accomplishment will increase and moreover, you will have peace of mind! You can't buy this, no matter how many raises and bonus checks you receive.

However, I understand. At the time, you likely needed a job, may have been desperate for a job and everything sounded good, looked good, the benefits were good, the pay may not have been all that great, but it was better than nothing, right? You likely had conversations and discussions with your friends, maybe your family about the position, but you never got around to having a conversation with the only One who could have let you know if this was the right move, at the right time in accordance with your purpose. Therefore, you blindly accepted the position and you have stayed one miserable year after another miserable year.

Being fired sometimes is the best thing that can happen to you. It doesn't feel good at the time, but if that's the only way to grab your attention and get you pointed in the right direction, God will sometimes cause you to be booted from where you are to take you to where you need to be, in order for you to become all He created you to become. In the in-between time — between losing what you had and landing in the place where you were meant to be — you will grow and mature in ways you never could have and never would have had you stayed stunted where you were. In addition to becoming a better person, you will likely end up in a better position. Perhaps you were meant to own and build your own business, not spend your time and waste your talents building up someone else's.

How long will you keep getting it wrong? You are running out of time and you are running out of options. If you are living a miserable existence, that is a good indication that you have been running in the wrong direction and it is time to change course.

Go back to the Master Craftsman and ask Him what He had in mind when He created you. Only He knows. Everyone else, including you, can only keep making bad guesses.

Giving Up Too Soon

We once had a houseplant that sat in the corner of our living room. I would move the plant from one corner to another corner of the room, trying to figure out in which corner it would look best. I finally moved the plant to my husband's home office. He could use a little greenery in there, I thought.

Shortly after moving the plant into his office, we noticed it had taken on a completely new life. The leaves became a rich green, it began to stand taller; and not only that, it began to sprout beautiful white blooms — blooms on top of blooms. We had seen a couple of small, sickly blooms before we moved it, but these were no comparison. They were hearty and strong. I learned they had been there all the time, on the inside, but couldn't fully blossom because we had the plant in the wrong environment.

This is the story for many of us. God knows what He has placed inside of us. He knows our potential because He placed it there. However, we have placed ourselves in the wrong environment and will never fully blossom until we are moved. When God wants to bless us and move us into our purpose, He will move us out of what has become a comfortable, though wrong environment, uproot us, and begin the painful process of changing and transforming us into that which He created us to become. He may isolate us and sometimes take us through what can be horrendous pain, humiliation, heartache, rejection, and failure — not to harm us, but to prepare us to step into our purpose and move on in our destiny.

Preparation is never pretty. It always comes in the form of adversity — storms, trials and tests — some of which can be so painful, the only way out, we think, is death. Even the great Apostle Paul, who wrote two-thirds of the New Testament was tested to the limit of his endurance when he wrote in 2 Corinthians 1:8, "For we do not want you *to* be unaware, brethren, of our affliction which came to *us* in Asia, that we were burdened excessively, beyond our strength, so that we despaired even of life."

I have earned a bachelor degree and a master degree from one of the finest universities in Texas and am working on a master's from one of the top seminaries in the world. I am not saying this to brag, but to make a personal point. None of those degrees prepared me for my purpose, adversity did. One local pastor calls it the University of Adversity — from which I have a Ph.D. I wouldn't be writing this book had I not gone through my own storms, trials and tests. I couldn't as effectively counsel depressed people, suicidal people, broke, busted and disgusted people who want to throw in the towel, thinking there is no way out other than a bullet to the head or by stuffing themselves with pills hoping not to wake up. This book isn't a product of my intellect but a product of my pain.

The same may be true for you. Could it be what you are going through is preparation? Stop being the honored guest at your own pity parties because what you are going through is not about you. It is to move you into a place of purpose and destiny so that you can become all you were designed to become, in order to enable you to reach back into the hellish existence of someone else and do the same for them.

If God is going to use you mightily, He is going to send you through some mighty tough stuff. This is why it is foolhardy to begrudge, be jealous and envious of people. You don't know their journey. If you did, it is doubtful you would have signed up for their assignment.

If you are going through unusually challenging times right now, I challenge you to change your perspective. It may be the lingering consequences of bad behavior but very likely it could be preparation. If you miss the meaning and the intent and give up too soon, you will never become all you were destined to become and you will end your life as a failure. I don't care how many accolades and beautiful tributes are said over your casket or how fat your bank account is when you die. You may die a rich and successful person by the world's standards. But if you failed to complete your God-given assignment it won't matter. You will have died a miserable failure in the eyes of the only One that matters.

PREPARATION

No one can know your pain, your shame,
the embarrassment you've brought to your hard-earned name.
You've raised the question a thousand times, "why?"
Now all you want is to fade away and die.
Even your most loyal and trusted friend,
has left you to twist alone in the wind.
Everything for which you've worked to achieve,
has been ripped away and it's hard to believe.
"How could this have happened?" You continually ask.
The answer I suggest can be found in the mask.
You know the mask I am referring to,
the one you wore to hide the real you.
You are hurting so badly because you had such pride,
now all is exposed, there is nowhere to hide.

Your image you thought, was everything and more,
but now you've been stripped right down to the core.
Those who have longed to see you fall,
are lapping it up and having a ball.
You had it all figured out or so you thought,
you had easily surpassed every goal you'd sought.
But God had a greater plan, you just couldn't see,
because you were trying on your own to be all you could be.
As great was your plan, His is far greater still,
and your status and influence are no match for His will.
God *will* accomplish what He has purposed to do,
even if it means lovingly breaking you.
And though this feels like total devastation,
it isn't at all. It's just preparation.
Once this is over, you will have a testimony.
You will be stronger and real, no longer a phony.
He is breaking you publicly to use you the same,
to show others the way and bring glory to His name.
What He wants you to learn during this time of sorrow,
is that He alone is your hope for tomorrow.
Recommit to God and give Him your *whole* heart.
He wants to give you a fresh, new start.
It hurts I know, because I have been where you are.
But left to our own, we can only go so far.
Someday you will look back and give thanks for this day,
because you will have known success — real success, God's
way.

IMBALANCED PERSPECTIVES

No matter who we are, no matter our race, culture, social status or profession, we all have the same human needs. Basic among them are food, clothing and shelter. Moreover, and to varying degrees, we all need to be loved, accepted, valued and respected.

When it comes to food, we can decide what to eat, when to eat and how much we want to eat. The same is true when it comes to clothing. Most of us have at least one closet; and depending upon our mood, occasion and the weather, we can decide what we want to wear, be it casual or dress; and, our wardrobes can be as simple or as extravagant as we can afford.

While there are those who for various reasons are unable to provide shelter for themselves, this is the exception and not the rule. For the majority of us, depending upon our lifestyle preference and bank account, we can live wherever we want and as simply or as luxuriously as we want. The bottom line is, we have choice and control.

The options of choice and control are powerful. So important, in fact, if taken away, many of us will go to extraordinary lengths or make extraordinary sacrifices to regain them — while the same is true if we feel we are about to lose them.

One reason it is difficult for many seniors to give up his or her car keys even when it becomes evident they can no longer operate a vehicle safely isn't because they are losing their cars, but losing their control.

Controlled needs are met needs because as long as it is within our power, purview and control to meet our own needs, we likely will not deny ourselves. While we can control how much or how little we eat, which brand of clothing to buy and where we want to live, what about the other needs — the needs we can't meet and control ourselves (i.e., love, acceptance, value, and respect)?

While food, clothing and shelter are physical — love, acceptance, value and respect are emotional. Mental health professionals will tell you that having a healthy and balanced view of ourselves is essential to having a healthy and balanced view of the world. Our view of the world and our view of people are filtered through the lenses of our experiences. For example, if you grew up in a household where your father cheated on your mother and was physically and verbally abusive, your view of marriage will be filtered through the tinted lenses of that tainted experience. Until you learn better, you will believe all men cheat and abuse their wives.

If you grew up in a household being told you were ugly, no good, unwanted, and shunned; you will grow up with low self-esteem and low self-worth. You could grow to become one of the most beautiful women or gorgeous men in town; yet, it won't matter how many people tell you that you are beautiful or good-looking, you won't believe them because when you look at yourself in the mirror, you are peering through the tinted lenses of your tainted life experiences. No amount of plastic surgery will change it because the problem isn't on your face, but in your mind. Our experiences determine what we believe, even when what we believe isn't true.

So, what does all of this have to do with forfeiting your purpose? I'm glad you asked. Our experiences determine the degree to which we need to be loved, accepted, valued and respected. If in our earlier experiences those needs were never adequately met, the relationships in which we later become involved — personal and professional — will suffer substantially because sometimes the void within can be so deep that enough will never be enough. No one will be able to love us enough, accept us enough, value us enough, or respect us enough to satisfy our need, regardless of how much he or she has proven otherwise. The problem however does not lie with them, but within us. This can strain the best relationships and if not properly addressed, will likely keep leading to less than pleasant parting of the ways. If professional, it could damage your career; if personal, your relationships — and could knock you off track for years to come.

On the other side of the coin is when we go overboard in attempting to meet this unhealthy, deep-seated and insatiable need for love, respect, value and acceptance. We will kiss babies and buns (not hot dog or hamburger), lie, cheat, and steal if we think it will satisfy one or more of these fragile needs. That's why people will among other things, claim degrees they haven't earned, drop names of people they don't know, pretend to be something they're not, wear ostentatious clothes and drive ostentatious cars when they can barely eke out a living while living in houses they can't afford. It is not about the things, but about being accepted and respected. The things are only a means to obtain these. It is a sure setup for a fall because pretenses are never permanent.

When the desperate, obsessive needs to be accepted, valued, respected, or loved take precedent in your life, you will lose sight of and abandon your purpose in hot pursuit of illegitimately satisfying them.

Keep a healthy perspective and gain a healthy balance. More important, get to know you, not the you behind the tinted lenses and not the one you have led people to believe you are. What drives us internally will be expressed externally because what is in always comes out and how it comes out determines our success or failure. Get to know your most intimate needs and how far you are willing to go and how much you are willing to give to satisfy them.

Our needs are legitimate. It is when we go about meeting them or having them met in illegitimate ways that we stumble and fall.

Enemies and Opposition — Count on it!

I can't conclude this chapter without stating the obvious. For believers this will not be new, but for others it may be. I want to make this as clear and as simple as I can. Whenever you begin to walk in your purpose, you are going to come under attack — guaranteed. I know some of you may not want to believe he exists, but I can't talk about God without talking about the enemy of God, and the enemy of mankind — Satan.

As a public official, I have served with and worked with a number of non-believers and agnostics, some are dear friends, but who nevertheless, choose to believe Satan is not real. Many put him right up there with the tooth fairy and the Easter bunny — Not! Satan *is* real. He is no joke and he is out to destroy you, destroy me, and to thwart the plan and purpose of God in our life. He is the antithesis of Jesus Christ, the Son of God. Jesus says in John 10:10, "The thief comes only to steal and kill and destroy; I came that they may have life and have *it* abundantly."

Satan would love for you to believe he isn't real because as long as you believe he isn't real, you will live your life as if he isn't real, apart from God; and tragically spend all of eternity discovering just how real he is.

The Apostle Peter refers to him as a roaring lion: "Be of sober *spirit*, be on the alert. Your adversary, the devil, prowls around like a roaring lion, seeking someone to devour" (1 Pet. 5:8).

The definition of devour is "to destroy, to swallow up, to consume; to prey upon voraciously."[2] Satan is a worthy adversary. You may be a genius, but you are no match for his ingenuity. You may be strong, but apart from God you are no match for his power.

Recall the definition of purpose from earlier in the chapter: Our purpose is to do that which God designed us to do through the optimal use of our talents and gifts, given to us by Him in order to glorify Him and be a blessing to others. Satan's goal is to stop that from ever taking place. God works *through* people to accomplish His divine plan. Satan works *through* people to oppose God's divine plan. He doesn't have the juice to destroy His plan, but he can so intimidate us, frustrate us, attack us, and cause us to fall into sin to the point where it will disqualify us from executing God's plan (i.e., our purpose). Even more, if we are not vigilant and know what to look for, he will sucker punch us every time. I know, because I have been sucker punched a time or two. So have we all whether we realize it or not.

How does he manage to do all of this under our nose and under the radar? Forget the pitchfork, red suit, tail, and horns bit — that *is* tooth fairy stuff. Satan does his destructive work through people — even at times, God-fearing church people. Okay, I won't go there, but tell the truth and shame the devil — it's true.

PERSEVERANCE — YOUR SECRET WEAPON

My 2007 city council campaign was particularly difficult, nasty, and brutal, but it made the victory that much sweeter. During the campaign, my friend and longtime campaign treasurer, Cheryl Washington, e-mailed to me a little story by Dr. Alan Zimmerman. It not only boosted my spirits at the time, but its message still ministers to me today:

A judge was campaigning for re-election and was running on his record of integrity. He was an honorable gentleman, but his opponent was conducting a vicious, mud-slinging, unfair campaign against him.

At a news conference, a reporter stood and asked the judge, "Your Honor, do you know what your opponent is saying about you? Are you aware of the criticism he is leveling at you? Would you care to comment?"

The judge looked at his campaign counselors and the chairman of his committee. Then he looked at his audience and calmly replied: "Well, when I was a boy I had a dog. And every time the moon was full, the old hound dog would howl and bark at the things he saw in the bright face of the moon. We never did sleep very well those nights. He would bark and howl at the moon all night long." With that, he concluded his remarks.

"That's beside the point," his campaign chairman impatiently said. "You haven't answered your critics!" The judge explained, "I just did! When the dog barked at the moon, the moon kept right on shining! I don't intend to say anything back to my critics. I'm going to keep right on shining — quietly and calmly, just like the moon!"

And you should do the same thing. When the difficult person is beating you down, just keep shining. Don't give him or her, the satisfaction of seeing you get down.[3]

Ask any successful person the keys to his or her success and chief among them will be their refusal to quit. The ability to persevere through hardships, addictions, devastating losses, disappointments, betrayals, rejections, loneliness, poverty, and pain separates the men from the boys, the women from the girls, the doers from the dreamers and the successful from the unsuccessful. You can't give up, quit, take your ball and go home because someone hurts your feelings or you failed the first time — even the second, third or fourth time.

If you know, that you know, that you know, what you're doing is what you were created to do, nobody can stop you. They may delay you, but they can't stop you because God is in control, not them. The beauty of it is He uses all of us in unique ways to accomplish His purposes — even wicked and evil people who are being used by the enemy in an attempt to stop you from fulfilling yours. "The LORD has made everything for its own purpose, Even the wicked for the day of evil" (Prov. 16:4).

If you give up and quit when the going gets tough, I have good news and I have bad news. The good news is that God is in the business of giving us new starts and new opportunities to complete our purpose. The bad news is that even in the fresh new starts and new opportunities the going is going to get tough. There is no way around it, but as Robert Frost once famously said, "The best way out is always through."

Below are the kinds of attacks you can count on and bank on that will come up against you. It is an all out assault from the enemy to force you to quit, to frustrate you to the point of quitting, or to frustrate you to the point of anger. Anger, borne out of frustration, is designed to cause you to strike out and strike back which will in the end make you look like the bad guy; and it is the bad guy — you, who will suffer the loss or forfeiture.

All of the below are designed to prevent you from fulfilling your God-given purpose. If you don't recognize them for what they are, you will never get past first base:

- Criticism

- Personal attacks

- Ridicule

- Rejection

- Insults

- Threats

- Intimidation

- Sabotage

- Fear

- Ambush

- False accusations

- Betrayal

- Character assassination

- Gossip

- Rumors

- Doubt

When you are attacked personally and your work is attacked publicly, stand firm and never quit. It is a good indication you are right where you are supposed to be. Like the judge in the story and as I have had to do many times more than I care to count — when attacked, keep shining!

The Master Craftsman has assigned to you a purpose and He has assigned it only to you, because you are the only one

He designed specifically to do it. Unlike Roy, don't get to the end of your run only to discover you have run the wrong way.

Talent is God given. Be humble. Fame is man-given. Be grateful. Conceit is self-given. Be careful.

—*John Wooden*

God hates a haughty look.

He says so in His Holy Book.

Don't get caught up in your money or bling

because in the end, they won't mean a thing.

Just when you think you've got it made

your bright star will begin to fade.

God shares His glory with no one at all.

Stay humble, if not, you're in for a fall.

CHAPTER 2

∽

ARROGANCE:
PRIDE CAN BE A BITTER PILL TO SWALLOW.

"...No one who has a haughty look and an arrogant heart will I endure."

Psalm 101:5

The story is told in Greek mythology of a young, strikingly handsome man named Narcissus. Narcissus was lean, but muscular. He had thick, beautiful hair and the kind of chiseled good looks that stopped women in their tracks. He was gorgeous from head to toe and by all accounts, smart, self-reliant, and successful. Narcissus was every woman's dream.

While none could match his flawless good looks, Narcissus would prove to be no match for his own fatal flaws — arrogance and vanity. Though many swooned at his feet and vied shamelessly for his affection, he would flippantly rebuff and callously reject without regard to others' humiliation and pain. He could care less how degraded he made them feel.

One day, unbeknownst to him, one of the broken-hearted prayed to the gods for vengeance — that Narcissus would know the pain of unrequited love, and that he too would experience the gut-wrenching agony of loving that which he could never possess. The goddess Nemesis heard the mournful prayer, and would soon answer it in the cruelest of ways.

Narcissus enjoyed an incredibly enviable lifestyle. However, he was obliviously unaware he had now been set up for a horrendous fall by someone whose love had grown cold with hatred.

Fiction is often a reflection of real life and in life as in this fictional account, people will often grow to hate what they cannot have — especially when they feel they have been arrogantly spurned, slighted, or used. The object of their affection then becomes the object of their venomous scorn.

One day while out hunting, Narcissus stumbled upon a hidden pool deep in the woods that was smooth like glass. He had grown thirsty and welcomed the opportunity to rest by the pool and take a long deep drink from the cool still waters. Little did he know it was a set up as Nemesis was about to answer that mournful, vengeful prayer.

Narcissus put down his gear and lay on his stomach at the edge of the pool with his face just above the surface as he prepared to take a refreshing sip. As he leaned further over the edge, he saw a reflection of his face on the surface of the water and he, like many who looked upon him, became instantly smitten. He fell fatally in love with the image of himself in the pool.

So deeply did Narcissus fall in love with his image, he could not bear to leave the edge of the pool, not even in search of food. Moreover, each time he would reach in to take a drink, the movement of the water created soft ripples which distorted his beloved image, so he dared not disturb the water even though his throat was increasingly parched with thirst.

For days on end, he lay mesmerized — longing for that which he could never have while growing progressively weaker from lack of food and water. Finally, one day, Narcissus quietly and sadly died — but not before having experienced fully, the kind of gut-wrenching pain he so arrogantly had caused so many others.[1]

Get Over Yourself

Arrogance is a shameless, prideful display of self-importance and superiority — a narcissistic view of one's self that has been, is, and always will be the genesis of some of the most crushing, publicly humiliating falls from grace. When we internalize external superficialities, attributes, and abilities — nurture them with ego, feed them with self-adoration, and allow them to swell our heads with pride, we become arrogant. Superficialities such as wealth, influence, power, fame, good looks, ability, heritage; all the way down to the cars we drive, the positions we hold and the houses in which we live can breed haughtiness and conceit. Moreover, our arrogance can turn once faithful friends into ruthless enemies.

In fact, sometimes the enemy is not a known enemy at all, but a business partner, best friend, colleague, or trusted employee. Those we least suspect are the ones that can hurt us most. Even sadder and more heartbreaking is we often don't discover the truth until after the fall.

It was Julius Caesar's close friend Brutus that helped plan, orchestrate, and execute the bloody assassination of the powerful Roman dictator. Caesar, like any astute leader, knew well his enemies and was always on guard against them. Never would he have suspected Brutus. After the savage attack, as blood and life drained from his body, he looked into the face of Brutus and uttered in dying disbelief, "Et tu, Brute?" You too, Brutus? Have you ever had a "you too, Brutus" experience? I have, and it can be devastating, especially when you go out of your way to give that person an opportunity when no one else would give them the time of day. The higher you rise; there will be a Brutus in the mix somewhere — guaranteed. Even Jesus had his — Judas. Think for a moment, who could be *your* Brutus?

Never get too high because there always will be a Brutus or a Judas scheming to bring you down. Like these two, they may be closer to you than you would like to think. Familiarity breeds contempt and it is often the silent contempt of seemingly supportive friends that drives their betrayal. Like Caesar, you will never see it coming.

Pass up the ride on the high horse because "pride goes before destruction, and a haughty spirit before stumbling," (Prov. 16:18). Arrogance sets into motion a series of events that when taken together will cause a hard fall. Tragically, there will be far fewer people around when we crash land as opposed to when we took flight; and fewer still who will stick around long enough to dig us from underneath the rubble of our imploded life.

THE HATERS

No matter how good-looking, wealthy or successful you may be, take care how you treat people. Haters never need a reason to hate, but the primary reasons haters hate are because they can't have what you have, do what you do, or be who you are. And it could be anyone — a disgruntled employee, political enemy, jilted lover or wanna-be lover. Even worse, a jealous colleague who feels you somewhere along the way rejected, belittled, ignored, disrespected, or got the position they felt they deserved and they will spend the better part of their lives seeking vengeance, revenge and your downfall. The longer you are in a position of authority, leadership, or in the limelight, the longer the list of haters grows.

They will lurk in the shadows, plotting secret revenge; at times colluding and scheming with others with whom but for a common enemy — you — they have little else in common. You'd be surprised at how people who may hate one another, but who hate you more, will become fast friends and close allies with the shared goal of bringing you down and destroying your life. You likely may not even remember their names or your supposed offense. However, they have never gotten past it and will never get over it.

Revenge is a powerful motivator and those hell-bent on getting back at you will make it their life's goal to hold you to account. Haters will obsessively spend their time tracking your career, covetously watching as you climb and succeed as they are left seething behind. Envy consumes them and anger fuels them because unlike you, no one has bothered to "give" them a break, let alone shower them with accolades and attention. What they don't understand, however, nor would they care to understand is that no one likely "gave" you anything.

They envy what you have without realizing what all it took for you to get it — long days, late nights, in other words, hard work. While they are unwilling to put in the work or make the necessary sacrifices, haters will blame you for their lack of success, even though you're not to blame for their miserable failures. They have come to believe that by now, had it not been for you, something you did or if you had not been in their way, they would be much further along. Haters view their failures as your fault.

Like the spurned lover who prayed for Narcissus's downfall, revenge-seekers are venomous, their plots deadly, and they are always looking for your Achilles heel. They will skillfully use your slightest misstep to turn others against you, sabotage your career, call into question your integrity and character; and, use any means at their disposal to damage or destroy your hard-earned reputation and credibility. Arrogance fuels the fire and exponentially boosts their incentive to bring you down hard.

So how do you avoid this insidiousness? First, let's dismiss the obvious. There will always be miserable people who live miserable lives who want to blame whomever they can for their miserable existence. The easiest people to blame and tear down are those in positions of leadership, authority and influence — even colleagues and neighbors whom they perceive are faring better, but especially those in the public eye whose success they somehow believe came at their expense. Whether you're arrogant or not, nothing will change this. However, because of arrogance, there are some things we bring upon ourselves that give some in their minds reason to seek retribution and revenge. Let's begin with the basic human needs to be respected, accepted, and valued.

What Goes Around Comes Around

In your climb to the top, take care not to stomp mud holes into the backs of others while on your way up. The imprints left by your hard-soled shoes of ambition will turn into indelible marks of resentment. Resentment gives birth to ugly twins — revenge and retaliation.

Moreover, simply because your position may afford you the opportunity, it does not give you the right to use people for selfish, business, or political gain, then toss them away like yesterday's trash. I realize this is contrary to the norm on any rung on the ladder of success where the dog-eat-dog mantra is always at a fevered pitch. However, I have learned one inescapable truth. Actually, I have learned a number of inescapable truths, but this one is worth the price of admission because it will spare you and those that care about you from so much shame and regret.

In politics, sports, religion, and business and in all of life, if you maliciously use someone, you will eventually *get* used by someone, but often in a more hurtful and humiliating way. Moreover, if you live, lead, or play on the public stage, it will come back to you on the public stage for the whole world to see. Whatever you throw out, will be thrown back at you; and whatever you dole out, will be doled back to you. Your actions are seeds, so be careful where you sow them. If you sow seeds of selfishness you are going to reap a crop of sorrow. It's the law of sowing and reaping and there are no exceptions. "Do not be deceived, God is not mocked; for whatever a man sows, this he will also reap" (Gal. 6:7).

It gets even better or worse depending upon how you look at it. Whatever you do in the dark will invariably come to the light, especially it seems if you have hypocritically held yourself out to be the avenger of evil, the model spouse; or, the stalwart of everything good, righteous and pure. Just be sure you are living by the same rules and standards by which you hold everyone else. If you are demanding certain behaviors of others, be sure to demand the same of yourself. Don't rain down fire and brimstone from the pulpit on adultery when you have a mistress sitting in the pews. Don't make your bones on the backs of those from whom you are secretly profiting. Otherwise, you will be caught with your pants down, your hand in the cookie jar, red-faced, and red-handed. A. L. Kitselman perhaps said it best, "The words 'I am' are potent words; be careful what you hitch them to. The thing you're claiming has a way of reaching back and claiming you."

Some people live to expose hypocrisy and the bigger the target, the higher the incentive. We have to walk the talk because no fall is more humiliating than that of one who preached, taught, or pretended one way and the covers were jerked away to reveal quite the opposite.

Never underestimate people. They may appear weak and small when you are at the top looking down, but never sell them short. Humans are remarkably resilient, persistent, and resourceful. Use people if you want, but don't be shocked when in the end, you are the one used.

TAKE TIME TO BE KIND

One of the greatest lessons to be learned from the tale of Narcissus and one of the greatest lessons I have learned is if you must sever a relationship, whether personal or professional, don't be high-handed or callous. Rather, do it in such a way that leaves the other person's dignity intact because that may be all they have left. Wouldn't you want the same?

Criticize a person's character, they can come back from that; sully their reputation, they can rebuild that; but destroy their dignity, and you strike at the heart of their self-worth. It is when people shamefully feel they have been reduced to nothing, with nothing left to lose, that they lose it. Nothing is more ominous than to find yourself in the cross hairs of a person who feels they have nothing to lose and even less for which to live.

If you habitually and haughtily strip away other's dignity because you are in a position to, for the sport of it; or, just to flex your muscle to show off, I can almost guarantee you that someone will be waiting for the opportunity to return the favor. Payback can be devastatingly wicked.

Narcissus had it all — good looks, influence and affluence. He rejected soundly those he found undesirable. But it wasn't so much that he rejected them; it was the manner by *which* he rejected them. You can endear people to you by giving them the grace to save face; or, risk incurring their wrath by deliberately putting them to shame. It is always best to respectfully reject and quietly dismiss. People have long memories. While they may forget what you said, they will never forget how they felt when you said it.

IT COULD ALL BE GONE OVERNIGHT

People admire confidence, but detest cockiness — especially in those whose source of cockiness is by virtue of a title or position they hold; and, one that can be easily stripped away at the next general election or next round of layoffs.

In the purest sense, position does not make the person any more than clothes make the man or woman. However, purity and politics just like purity and business make for oxymoronic fairytales. In both, it is always about the position, rarely about the person. If you believe otherwise, you are in for a serious ego-buster. The sad reality is whether in the everyday world of work, in the high stakes world of business, or in the heady world of politics; if you don't rank, you don't matter.

Without regard to how good a person you may be, in those worlds you are only as good as your position. If you don't believe that, consider this. If you think you are included on the A-list and in the inner circle because of who you are, rather than because of the position you hold or the influence you wield, lose your next political campaign; be removed from the influential board post; get indicted or get booted from your firm.

The invitations to social events will slow to a trickle, your telephone calls won't be returned as quickly, if at all, and you will soon discover that life as the former CEO, former mayor, fallen pastor or whatever title or position you held that caused you to arrogantly believe that it was all about you — is anything but fun. It is tough being an insider on the outside looking in or a star player with no team for which to play. Your boss, colleagues, or teammates will abide your arrogance — even attitude — while demonstrating high levels of tolerance, great degrees of patience, and artificial affection for as long as they need you. However, when they no longer need you, you will be discarded like a wet newspaper.

IMAGINE THIS

This is so elementary that it is frequently missed — as you climb steadily upward, don't burn bridges you may need to cross again and never cross people you may need again. Life has a way of bringing you back to those same bridges and those same people. Stay grounded and true to those who trust you. Moreover, stay true to yourself and not try to live up to some hyped up image that can so easily become distorted and ultimately destroyed.

Image is the root word of imagine. The image you project is a reflection of who and what you imagine yourself to be. That is not necessarily a bad thing. However, when you imagine that you are far superior, more attractive, more brilliant, or more entitled than any of your peers and colleagues, and snobbishly act it out as though it were true — that's arrogance. On the other hand, you can be genuine, selfless, and without pretense — leading, guiding, and serving others with excellence, humility, and grace — that's smart. You can be arrogant and smart, but if you are smart, you won't be arrogant.

Narcissus died at the place where he became enamored with his image at the expense of substance. The same will figuratively happen to you and me when all that matters is our image and not our substance. It's not *what* people believe we are, but *who* we are that matters. If you have built your life around the smoke and mirror of your image be careful, because when the smoke clears and the mirror cracks, people will discover that you aren't all you were cracked up to be and the fall from grace will be brutal.

You may not notice it right away; in fact, it may take years. But it is an irrefutable fact of human existence. Arrogance builds the ego as it rots the soul. An inflated ego is a deceptive diversion — an illusion which makes you believe you are more important than you actually are, more brilliant than you actually are, and less destructible than you have been built up to believe. Arrogance is no laughing matter and the last laugh will likely be at your expense.

The Last Laugh

Jack Abramoff was once one of the most powerful lobbyists in Washington, D.C. He was at the heart of one of the furthest reaching corruption scandals in Capitol history. Mr. Abramoff came to symbolize major scale corruption and back room dealings between powerful politicians and high-octane lobbyists. The scandal rocked Capitol Hill and the White House.

According to an Associated Press story at his sentencing hearing, Mr. Abramoff said this as he stood before the court, "I come before you as a broken man. I'm not the same man who happily and arrogantly engaged in a lifestyle of political and business corruption."[2]

What he uttered later, however, was more sobering. He said, "My name is the butt of a joke, the source of a laugh and the title of a scandal." No laughing matter, this easily could be the unintentional sum total of any of our lives. Arrogance will cause us to laugh with pride today, but weep in shame tomorrow.

When arrogance and vanity becomes our signature, we are setting ourselves up for the most embarrassing, painful and shameful fall of them all. Why does this one hurt the most, and is the most embarrassing? Simple, God hates pride and He will bring down the haughty and high-minded every time, and often in the most humiliating and public way.

Should you be confident in who you are and be proud of your accomplishments? Absolutely. Just don't get the big head and think you have accomplished what you have alone. You haven't. You could say you are a self-made man or woman. Okay, but who created the "self" you claim to have made? You had to start with something — like a mind and a body, maybe? Where did those come from? You? Of course not. No one is self-made. Every talent, skill, gift, and ability we have comes from God — every one of them. So how can we get puffed up over attributes, gifts, and talents that we had no hand in creating? We may have improved upon them, but if they were never there, there would be nothing upon which to improve. Get the idea?

Arrogance has cost millionaires their fortunes, professional athletes their careers, leaders and preachers their reputations, executives their positions and everyday people their livelihoods;

and, has left a trail of wrecked lives, broken marriages, and damaged families.

"God is opposed to the proud, but gives grace to the humble" (James 4:6, 1 Pet. 5:5). Stay humble, because pride can be a bitter pill to swallow.

I think we all have a little voice inside us that will guide us. It may be God, I don't know. But I think that if we shut out all the noise and clutter from our lives and listen to that voice, it will tell us the right thing to do.

- Christopher Reeve

Even at the time, it was an uneasy choice.

But I wanted what I wanted, so I ignored the voice.

That small, inner voice with which we are born

is designed to protect, prevent, and warn.

I wish I had listened that fateful day.

But I refused to give in, I wanted my way.

I'm now paying the price because I chose to ignore

that still small voice, my conscience — my core.

~✑

CHAPTER 3

IGNORING THE CORE:
THE TENSION OF PASSION AND CONSCIENCE

"Blessed are those who have a tender conscience, but the stubborn are headed for serious trouble."

Proverbs 28:14; NLT

There is a one-sentence life lesson many of us learned in grade school — "Always let your conscience be your guide."[1] We don't hear this much anymore. In the politically correct world of politics, me-first world of business, and prima donna world of professional sports, there is little regard for absolutes. Fundamental truths rooted in decency, honesty, ethics, morality and respect — once gold standards have become seemingly rusty relics of days gone by. Once the backbone of behavior and barometer of integrity, they have been relegated to the backbench of today's busy lives. As a result, too many of us are swayed by what feels right, no matter how wrong, and live by what makes us feel good, rather than what is good for us.

Our conscience, that built-in moral compass designed to serve as both a warning device and navigational system to help us determine right from wrong; and, to guide us toward or away from the same, has become for many, jaded, seared, sadistically dysfunctional, and for still others, totally disengaged. This is especially troublesome for those who are keepers of the public's trust: those that hold the livelihood of others in the palm of their hand, and those whose very actions and words determine the fate of others. "Trust that man in nothing who has not a conscience in everything," said novelist Laurence Sterne.

Politics was once one of my greatest passions. In reference to those in politics, as it relates to conscience, Mary Beth Rogers in her book, *Barbara Jordan: American Hero,* quotes the late Congresswoman thusly, "You need a core inside you," Jordan said. "A core that directs everything you do. You confer with it for guidance. It is not negotiable. No amount of money will make you violate the core. If you don't have that, then forget about elective politics. If you do, then it will guide you well."

I can't help but wonder what the revered Congresswoman would think if she were alive today. What she would find would be a political landscape littered with the decaying carcasses of once promising political careers — dead careers which were guided not by core but misguided by greed and deception.

If you are a leader and if people are depending upon *you* to guide *them*, what are *you* depending upon to guide you? Rules? Regulations? Rules and regulations are good, but principles are better. Principles have deeper roots than rules because principles define the essence of who we are. They are the offshoot of our consciences. Rules are developed by people to govern and control. The conscience is instilled by God to guide and reprove. It sounds the alarm when we are about to make dangerous choices and convicts us when we do wrong.

While our conscience is our moral compass, it isn't always programmed by moral people. In fact, many people who have never opened a Bible, never read one scripture, or even set foot inside a church intrinsically know right from wrong. Even more, some live cleaner lives with clearer consciences than some Christians live; and, would never dream of doing on occasion what some of us do as a matter of routine.

All of us are products of systems, first our family, then a succession of systems or groups with which we choose to be part (i.e., social, political, religious, non-religious, etc.). Our conscience is shaped by the beliefs of the people or systems that influence us along the way, particularly during our formative years. Sigmund Freud maintained that our conscience, developed by age five, is shaped by the moral and ethical influences of parents and caregivers.

My set of moral values was shaped by Christian influences. Your set of moral values is set and programmed by your influences as well. Moreover, we gravitate to, and are more comfortable in, those environments where our set of moral values line up with people of like moral values. This is the problem I have with people who lump people together by skin color rather than by shared values; or, those who lay guilt trips on people because they are acting outside of what in their opinion is the acceptable way — given their race — they should think, act, talk, and feel. When are we going to get a revelation, Christians included, that just as blood is thicker than water, values are deeper than skin?

If you grew up in a household where stealing was the acceptable norm, and those around you stole, then robbing a bank or stealing a purse wouldn't prick your conscience at all. In fact, it would be in silent agreement because that was how it was programmed. Does it excuse the behavior? Of course it doesn't. However, it does explain how you could steal with impunity and not feel a twinge of guilt. Our conscience only warns and convicts when it has been programmed based upon the moral law of God, standards, principles, and acceptable mores of the society in which we live. Combined, these work together to calibrate our conscience. God gave to us all the wonderful gift of conscience.

Our conscience was designed to work as a warning device and a navigational system to sound the alarm when we are about to violate any part of our set of values. And, it sets boundaries for our thoughts, emotions, and behavior. It also gives us an emotional understanding of morality. Our choices and decisions are limited by our conscience. An ill-programmed conscience or one in need of serious calibration will have a warped sense of limits and boundaries. When this is the case, a downfall looms. Because of our intellect and the capacity to reason and excuse, boundaries are a necessity. Without the tug of guilt initiated by our conscience when we are about to violate an established boundary, we will revert to our most common and lowest denominators to dictate our behavior — feelings and instincts. As such, we will do what feels good, never mind that it is far from good for us. God gave us a conscience to save us from ourselves.

Having My Cake and My Conscience Too

Psychologist and best-selling author John Gray, in his book, *Children Are From Heaven* said, "Developing the mind is important, but developing a conscience is the most precious gift parents can give their children."

It has been shown that babies as young as six months use deception to get what they want. If you have children, you are aware of how easily we can sometimes be manipulated by them. Most of the time not maliciously, but that's just how children are. They, like us, want what they want and can be very self-centered and manipulative. Unless a child is taught right from wrong based upon absolute truth (i.e., the Word of God), self-centered and manipulative children grow up to become self-centered and manipulative adults. As a result, they end up with shipwrecked lives, and will wonder how they ended up stranded on the beach of a bankrupt life when their goal was to set sail for the high seas of success. As parents, we owe them better.

My late aunt and uncle raised my brothers, sisters, and me as foster children in the small East Texas town of Jefferson. They were both schoolteachers and active, highly respected people of the community. It was the kind of community where everyone knew everyone. The adults had a strong sense of right and wrong, and were not at all shy about disciplining not only their children, but also anyone else's children if they got out of line in their presence. They would be sure to tell the parents of the kid they disciplined so the parents could do the same once they got home. There would be no discussion, no time out, none of that stuff. You got paddled for doing wrong and then got paddled for having to be paddled for doing wrong. It was as if the adults were silent conspirators with a communication and spy network to rival that of the FBI. If you sneezed, someone told your parents about it. What today is considered child abuse was then considered discipline — even more, the development of character and conscience.

One sunny spring afternoon, while in elementary school, I walked with my aunt (Aunt Leo) to the tiny mom and pop grocery located just across the street from the school where she taught and I attended. I had never seen so many goods and gadgets. Aunt Leo went to the back of the store, but, before stepping away, told me to stay put at the front counter. I did — for a while. However, with the wide-eyed fascination of a child, the tug of curiosity became too great and I took a few timid steps away from the glass-topped wooden counter to peer around a stack of canned goods to see how far away Aunt Leo was so I could make a clean get-away.

Satisfied she was a safe distance away, I began to venture around this strange, but appealing place. I walked slowly through the aisles, stopping at times to look more closely at some of the wares, fascinated by it all. As I made my way back to the front of the store, I saw them — my favorite snack cakes, small, round two-layered, chocolate moist cakes soft and stuffed with creamy white filling. Individually wrapped in cellophane, they sat eye-level on the shelf, snuggled between the honey buns and frosted cinnamon rolls.

Not knowing any better, I picked up one of the cakes and thought to myself, *what a treat!* By then, I could hear Aunt Leo's voice as she laughed and talked with an acquaintance. Judging by the distance of her voice and the click of her heels against the wooden floor, I could tell she was heading back to the front counter. I dashed up the aisle, rounded the corner just in time, and was waiting at the counter as she walked up. My only hope was that she couldn't hear me panting from the mad dash, and out of fear that she somehow may have known I had wandered away. Thankfully, she hadn't noticed. She concluded her business, thanked the storekeeper and we walked out of the store and headed back to the school. Neither of them noticed that in my hand, was the little chocolate cake.

It was a beautiful day. I had my favorite treat in the entire world and my aunt held my hand as I skipped across the street. When we crossed the street, I let go of her hand so I could take the wrapping off my luscious chocolate cake. As I took the first savory bite, Aunt Leo stopped walking, looked down at me and asked sternly, "Where did you get that?" "At the store we just came from," I replied. "Who gave you the money to buy it?" She continued. I was thinking to myself as I gulped down the first bite, *money, what money?* "Nobody, I just picked it up while I was waiting for you," I said innocently.

I could tell as the color drained from her face that I was in major trouble. She would now know that I had left the counter after she told me to stay put. I couldn't have known there was a much bigger issue at hand. I did sense, however, that my goose was cooked. Little did I know however, that I was about to learn a lesson I would never forget and one that would serve me well many years down the road.

Aunt Leo was a tall woman. Looking up at her that day, it seemed as if she had grown at least five feet since we had left the store! She narrowed her eyes and ordered me to stop eating my prized little cake. We walked in hurried silence to the principal's office (always a bad sign for any kid, even if your parent is a teacher at the school). She told the principal she needed someone to cover her class for a few minutes and to tell my teacher that I was with her. *Okay, this is it,* I thought to myself. She's going to kill me for sure and I would never see my sisters and friends again!

As we trudged along the same path we had taken earlier, the sun didn't seem so bright and the day not as beautiful. It was as if a dark cloud enveloped us as we silently walked. Still not quite sure what all the fuss was about, she stopped and glared at me with those dark, deep-set eyes and said, "Dorothy, what you did was stealing. Stealing is one of the worst things you can do. If you lie, you'll steal and if you steal, you'll lie. Don't you ever, I don't care how old you are, or where you end up in life, don't ever take anything that don't belong to you, and don't ever take anything you didn't work for, ever! We're going back over to that store, you're going to give this cake back to that man, tell him you took it without paying for it, and tell him you're sorry and you'll never do it again. Do you understand me girl?" "Yes ma'am," I muttered.

It felt as though I had been kicked in the stomach. The sweet taste remaining in my mouth from the first bite of the cake had turned bitter. As we reached the store, the last thing I wanted to do was go back in with her and do as she had ordered. I was so ashamed. But the choice wasn't mine to make. Aunt Leo marched me up to that storekeeper who was standing behind the very counter from which I wished I had never slipped away. She told him I had something to say. I handed him the partially wrapped, partially eaten cake and between tears, gasps and gulps for air, managed to say every word Aunt Leo told me to say. I remember his kind eyes as the two of them exchanged glances.

I never learned his name and I suppose it never mattered. He pulled his glasses down on his nose, leaned across the counter, peered down at me over the black rimmed glasses and with the kindest, warmest smile, he said, "Little girl, you've just paid me more than that cake could ever be worth." He handed it back to me, patted my hand and said, "Go ahead and keep it." I looked at Aunt Leo, she gave me a terse smile and nod, and I managed to whisper a hushed, "thank you."

Aunt Leo thanked him and as we turned to leave, I looked back at the balding storekeeper with the crisp white apron as he busied himself with another customer. As my aunt and I neared the door, we walked past bushels of produce. Someone no doubt would later wonder, as they picked through the fresh fruits and vegetables, how a partially wrapped, partially eaten little chocolate cake ended up tucked gently between the baskets. Even though the storekeeper told me to keep it, something inside told me differently.

Decades have passed since that fateful day. Aunt Leo and the gentle storekeeper have long since passed away. However, the lessons they taught me that day and the conscience they helped develop endures.

As of this writing, I am completing my fourth term on the town council. During one campaign for office, I received a call from an area developer with longstanding ties to many of my colleagues. He wanted to meet with me and help with my campaign. We met, and as we ended the meeting, he walked me to my car and handed me a sealed envelope. I thanked him, we said our good-byes, and I drove away. A mile or two down the road, I stopped at a red light, glanced over at the envelope I had carelessly tossed onto the passenger seat. I picked it up, ripped it open and nearly gagged when I saw it had been stuffed with $100 bills with a list of names of "contributors" I did not know and was certain did not know me. The contribution was well over the "legal" limit, but since it was broken down by individual contributors, it technically was "legal."

I had that "kicked in the stomach" feeling again and I don't know when the signal light turned green, but I was startled back to reality at the blaring of car horns as the guy in the faded red pickup behind me saluted me with his middle finger.

I hurried home, desperately uneasy, and called a more experienced colleague seeking advice. He thought the whole thing was comical, assured me it was "perfectly legal" and nonchalantly said, "Dorothy, we all do it." *Really*, I thought, as I thanked him and put down the receiver. Since I wanted to be like everyone else in this game to which I was new, I decided to keep the money.

I reported the contribution as required by Texas elections laws. However, over a period of several days, I began being haunted by memories from that sunny afternoon so many years ago and somehow felt as if I had stolen the little chocolate cake all over again. I hadn't thought of this in years. Even though the contribution skirted local campaign and reporting rules, it was technically legal I rationalized. However, I knew deep down that keeping it would be morally wrong. I set aside the ripped envelope for the duration of the campaign and justified keeping the money by reminding myself, *That's just how the game is played Dorothy, get used to it.*

The campaign ended. I won the race. However, I was still faced with what to do with the envelope of cash. Surely, I told myself, there is no harm in keeping the money now. I could throw a party for my friends and supporters. I could bank it or use it to reimburse myself for out-of-pocket campaign expenses. My conscience wasn't buying any of it. I knew I would have no peace until I returned every penny.

One weekend afternoon, a week or so after the campaign ended, I looked up the developer's home address, gave him a call, and asked if I could come over. He agreed. As I drove from my house to his, I experienced the same feeling I had crossing the street with Aunt Leo to take back the little chocolate cake — one of dread. I pulled off the street, onto his driveway and I knew then, there was no turning back. As I slowly trudged to the front door, I felt a range of awkward emotions.

He invited me in and we sat and talked for a few minutes. I then got down to the reason for my visit. I first expressed my gratitude for the financial support, and then took out the new envelope in which I had placed the cash. I set it on the coffee table. Since I am sensitive about appearing ungrateful, this made my task all the more difficult. I somehow got through it and then it was his turn to talk. He said in all of his years in business they had contributed thousands to numerous elected officials in the area and this was new to him — not one had ever returned a contribution.

We made more small talk. By then, we both were breathing a little easier. At the end, we stood up and shook hands. I thanked him again. As I walked out of the door, it felt as if a boulder had been lifted from my shoulders. I climbed back into my SUV. As I drove away, I let down the windows, opened the sunroof, and as I breezed down the narrow two-lane road, I couldn't help but think that through the opened roof, Aunt Leo was smiling down saying, "You didn't forget after all."

The Compromised Core

In a world that celebrates an individual's right to do whatever makes him or her happy, who is to say my right isn't your wrong and your wrong isn't my right? Moreover, if my truth is my truth and your truth is your truth, which one of our truths is true?

The only truth that has never changed and will never change is the truth of God's Word. It is the uncompromising standard. Its absolutes are unchangeable whether we agree with them or not, choose to ignore them, or believe them or not. His word doesn't vacillate with the political winds. In the end, we all are going to be judged by the same standard. And heeding our conscience's warnings not only will prevent us from stumbling, but will protect us from violating the standard to which we will all someday be held accountable.

So hard-wired is our conscience, that once developed, it takes conscious effort to ignore and disable it. Our core doesn't become compromised overnight nor can it be corrupted without our consent. Corrosion of a healthy conscience begins by acting on an illegitimate want with the silent consent of a legitimate will. The two work in tandem because a want without the will to act upon it, is nothing more than a wish. Wishes are harmless. Acting upon wants, unhampered and unfettered by an undisciplined, out of tune conscience, can spell the end of our career and sully a sterling reputation. When left to our lowest common denominators of human behavior, there is no limit to the depths to which we can plunge.

Our conscience shapes our character. The depth of our conscience determines the breadth of our character. Show me a person with no conscience and I will show you a person with no character. What's more, one whose downfall is imminent. The higher we climb, the more wealth, power, and influence we attain, the more difficult it becomes to listen to that still, small voice. Nevertheless, never get so high that no one, not even your conscience, can tell you no.

If we resist what at times can be powerful temptations to ignore it, that little voice will keep us from being caught up in dirty deals and scandalous situations that will ruin our careers and lives. It will prevent us from stumbling headlong into an affair that will ultimately destroy our family and ruin our reputation. Even more, it will protect us from engaging in shameful hypocrisy. We don't often consider our conscience as saving us from hypocrisy, but it will.

Hypocrisy can do as much damage to our reputation and credibility as any illicit act and can cause even more embarrassment and humiliation. Listen to your conscience before opening your mouth to rail against people or situations which you piously and self-righteously hold yourself out to be the lead crusader against, but ones in which you are secretly engaging. Our conscience knows our secrets, tendencies and motives.

It will not only keep us from doing things we shouldn't do, but from saying things we shouldn't say, particularly when we are engaging in the very thing we are railing against.

If you're a male leader who enjoys railing against homosexuality, be sure you don't have a closeted boyfriend. If you rain down fire and brimstone on adultery, make sure you're not sneaking too. Someone is always watching and someone will always tell. If we allow it, our conscience will be the first to tell — not to harm or embarrass but to prevent us from making fools of ourselves. It will then be up to us to make corrections in our behavior before it is too late. Our conscience will not force us to change. It will only make us aware that there is a need to change. What we choose to do about it is up to us. It will never browbeat us into submission.

THE ANATOMY OF DISENGAGEMENT

Our conscience does not stop working without our consent. It does not become disengaged without our effort. Disengagement is not instantaneous. It comes over time and in phases. From my experience, there are seven phases we go through before our conscience disengages:

PHASE I — A THOUGHT —
Our Conscience Sounds the Alarm

Every action is preceded by a thought, if nothing but an impulsive one. It has been estimated the average person has between 12,000 and 60,000 thoughts per day. The thoughts upon which we dwell are the ones we will more likely take action on. For example, if a guy meets and sees the same beautiful woman enough times, and he thinks about her for any length of time, it won't be long before he asks her out. If he or she is married, that may just be nothing more than a minor inconvenience. Men are visual, and they visualize well before they make a move. It is at the point of taking action that the conscience will sound the alarm.

Whether we think long and hard about a person, a piece of jewelry, or item of clothing we want to buy (that we know we can't afford); the longer we dwell on those thoughts, the higher the likelihood we will eventually act upon them. That is why in Philippians 4:8, the Apostle Paul gives us a whole laundry list of things on which to allow our mind to dwell. It takes conscious effort to change our thoughts especially when they are tied to a perceived want or need.

PHASE II — ACTION –
OUR CONSCIENCE SCREAMS NO! SWIFTLY CONVICTS

"I can't believe I did that!"

"How could have I done such a thing?"

"Lord, please forgive me. I promise not to do that again."

"I'll buy her that ring she's been wanting since Christmas."

If we ignore the early warnings and willfully override our conscience's efforts to point out the error of our thoughts, we will act upon what we have been dwelling upon. And depending upon the calibration of our conscience, guilt will be minor or gut wrenchingly painful. But there will be guilt. If our actions are revolting enough to us, we will be more inclined to nip them in the bud during this phase and not allow things to progress. If we decide to overrule our conscience in Phase I and act on our thoughts in Phase II, it is still not too late to reverse course. In fact, this is the ideal point to reverse course. If we don't nip it here, it becomes much more complicated and convoluted as time passes and we become more comfortable in ignoring the warnings.

PHASE III — SELF-ANGER —
OUR CONSCIENCE SAYS NO AND CONVICTS

"Why do I keep doing this?"

"I can't keep doing this!"

"What is wrong with me?"

"Why am I such a bonehead?"

"I hate myself. I swear this is it this time!"

We didn't stop in Phase II, and we become angry and frustrated with ourselves for being so weak and once again giving in. We know we are better than what we are doing. We will hate the fact that we keep doing it and hate the fact that we keep lying to others, and even worse, to ourselves. We will swear to stop, but each time it gets easier and easier. It is during this phase that we begin to make decisions that could impact our lives for some time to come.

PHASE IV — JUSTIFICATION –
OUR CONSCIENCE GROWS FAINT

"If my wife would fix herself up, I wouldn't have to do this. I told her to lose the weight!"

"I don't want to keep sleeping with my boss, but he appreciates me more than my husband."

"If they would pay me what I'm worth, I wouldn't have to take money off the top."

"It's not a bribe; I give so much of my time to this community, I deserve this!"

"My dad was like this, why should I be any different?"

This is the point of defiance and rebellion. We have made up our minds that the course we're on is the course we want to be on, are going to stay on, and no one is going to tell us differently. We are not interested in listening to our conscience or taking any friendly advice from family or friends. Phase IV begins the long slide downward because it is at this point we willfully and deliberately tune out our conscience. The point where we begin defensively justifying wrong actions is the point when our conscience grows faint to the point of near silence. It will no longer sound the alarm, tell us no, or fight our resistance. That's one thing our conscience will never do. It will never get into a boxing match with us. It warns, it guides, it admonishes, but it never fights. Rather, the still small voice grows fainter and fainter until it decreases to a tiny whisper and finally falls silent.

PHASE V — AGREEMENT —
Our Conscience Grows Ever So Faint

*"This is just who I am. Whoever doesn't like it,
    it's their problem, not mine."*

*"It's nobody's business what we do.
    My marriage was over a long time ago anyway."*

*"Who needs them? We can start all over again.
    We were meant to be together."*

*"As long as I'm here, I might as well take as much
    as I can get."*

*"I don't need any counseling. I know exactly what
    I'm doing and I'm loving every bit of it!"*

This phase marks, for the first time, the cataclysmic point whereby our illegitimate feelings come into full agreement and alignment with our illegitimate actions. There is no more guilt, doubt, self-anger, or any feelings contrary to the Agreement Phase. All of you is in full agreement with this new reality. It becomes your new normal. The volume level of our conscience during this phase is barely above a whisper.

PHASE VI — DISENGAGEMENT —
Our Conscience Falls Silent

The little voice falls silent. The needle on our compass is stilled and we begin the descent into decadence. Novelist and poet Samuel Butler said it best, "Conscience is thoroughly well-bred and soon leaves off talking to those who do not wish to hear it."

Absent the conscience, we are left to our lowest common denominator. Our feelings will give us permission to do whatever we want, whenever we want, however we want, how often we want and with whomever we want — without regard to guilt or shame or how our actions affect the lives of those around us. The one remaining boundary is rock bottom.

PHASE VII — THE FALL

Behavior without the constraint and conviction of our conscience can lead to an astonishing fall. Heeding our conscience's warning is a decision of the will. Ignoring it is a decision we will live to regret. How many times can we look back and say to ourselves things such as:

"I wish I had followed my first mind."
"Deep down, something told me to wait to get married."
"All the signs were there, I just didn't pay any attention."
"I wish I had listened. Something told me to stay home that night."
"I should have just walked away like something told me to."

We can all make one or more of these kinds of hindsight statements. So, why don't we listen to that small, still voice? Is it ego? Is it arrogance? It is some of all of that. However, I would venture to say it can be summed up in a word we don't hear much anymore, but is characteristic of many of us when it comes to obedience of any kind — stubbornness. We simply don't like being told no, even if the no is a whisper and not a shout; and, for our own good.

We want what we want. "With God all things are possible" (Matt. 19:26) has given way to "with credit cards and the Internet all things are possible." We will not be denied, and when we make up our mind to do something our conscience is warning us not to do; or buy something our conscience is telling us we can't afford, our emotions, will, and ***buts*** kick into overdrive:

> *"I know I should leave now and go home, **but**…"*
> *"I know I shouldn't take this money, **but**…"*
> *"I know I should stop sleeping with him, **but**…"*
> *"I know I can't pay for this right now, **but**…"*
> *"I know I'm supposed to be home by midnight, **but**…"*

Whenever you find yourself making these kinds of statements, pay close attention. When you follow up what you know to be true with a *but* in order to justify what you want to do, beware. What you do on the other side of the *but* may very well be your undoing — no matter how innocent, good or right it may appear at the time.

Back up, change directions, and follow your compass because *buts,* a lot of the time, are but set ups for a fall. The less we rely on our conscience and the more we rely on our feelings and emotions, the greater the odds we will be swayed by how good someone or something looks or how good he, she, or it makes us feel.

A Clear Conscience

How can you keep your conscience clear? Do what you know is right. Each time we deliberately ignore our conscience, our hearts become hardened. As a result, over a period of time, our capacity to tell right from wrong diminishes and our desire to do what is right lessens. While the above phases seem cut and dried, they aren't. Sometimes we can find ourselves with one foot in one phase, with the other foot in another. However, they are meant to give you a general idea of what phase of disengagement you may now find yourself. With each phase, the voice grows fainter and fainter. It is dangerous to be left to unrestrained emotions with the ability and opportunity to act on them at will without the consequence of conscience.

As we start down that slippery slope, at first we feel the small tugs and gnawing sense of wrong as the little voice softly continues to warn. As we persist, the voice will grow fainter and after awhile, we won't feel quite so guilty. What once was abnormal becomes our new normal. What we once abhorred we now enjoy. What we once condemned in others we now approve and do ourselves. Ultimately, what was wrong becomes right.

Don't start down this slope because it is a long and difficult trek back up. No matter who you are, billionaire or blue collar, don't ignore your core. It's trying to tell you something. The question however is, are you listening?

The end of an ox is beef, and the end of a lie is grief.

- African Proverb

There is no such thing as an innocent lie.

Someone will get hurt, or something will die.

Nothing may happen at all right away,

but there always will be a reckoning day.

A cover up is a set up for an embarrassing fall.

You could lose everything — you could lose it all.

Many have taken this road before.

Once they were... but they are no more.

CHAPTER 4

∼

LYING:
LIES ARE CHEAP — BUT MAINTENANCE AND
AFTERMATH ARE COSTLY.

"He who speaks truth tells what is right, But a false witness, deceit."

Proverbs 12:17

A folktale from India tells of a king who, during the day, used to sit on his throne and dispense justice, but who at night was accustomed to disguise himself and to wander about the streets of his city looking for adventures.

One evening he was passing by a certain garden when he observed four young girls sitting under a tree conversing together in earnest tones. Curious to overhear the subject of their discourse, he stopped to listen.

The first said, "I think of all tastes the pleasantest in the world is the taste of meat."

"I don't agree with you," said the second. "There is nothing so good as the taste of wine."

"No, no," cried the third, "you are both mistaken, for of all tastes the sweetest is the taste of love."

"Meat and wine and love are all doubtless sweet," remarked the fourth girl. "But in my opinion nothing can equal the taste of telling lies."

The girls then separated and went to their homes. And the king, who had listened to their remarks with lively interest and with much wonder, took note of the houses into which they went, and, having marked each of the doors with chalk, he returned to his palace.

The next morning he called his vizier (chief minister), and said to him, "Send to the narrow street, and bring before me the owners of the four houses, the doors of which have a round mark in chalk upon them."

The vizier at once went in person, and brought to the court the four men who lived in the houses to which the king had referred. Then said the king to them, "Have not you four men four daughters?"

"We have," answered they.

"Bring the girls hither before me," said the king.

But the men objected, saying, "It would be very wrong that our daughters should approach the palace of the king."

"Nay," said the king, "if the girls are your daughters, they are mine too, besides which, you can bring them privately."

So the king sent four separate litters (a hand-carried or animal-carried carriage), curtained in the usual manner, and the four girls were thus brought to the palace and conducted (escorted) into a large reception room. Then he summoned them one by one to his presence as he required them.

To the first girl he said, "O daughter, what were you talking about last night when you sat with your companions under the tree?"

"I was not telling tales against you, O king," answered she.

"I do not mean that," said the king. "But I wish to know what you were saying."

"I merely said," replied she, "that the taste of meat was the pleasantest."

"Whose daughter, then, are you?" inquired the king.

"I am the daughter of a Bhábrá," answered she.

"But," said the king, "if you are one of the Bhábrá tribe, who never touch meat, what do you know of the taste of it? So strict are they, that when they drink water they put a cloth over the mouth of the vessel, lest they should swallow even an insect."

Then said the girl, "Yes, that is quite true, but, from my own observation, I think meat must be exceedingly pleasant to the palate. Near our house, there is a butcher's shop, and I often notice that when people buy meat, none of it is wasted or thrown away. Therefore, it must be precious. I also notice that, when people have eaten the flesh, the very bones are greedily seized upon by the dogs, nor do they leave them until they have picked them as clean as a lance head. And even after that, the crows come and carry them off, and when the crows have done with them, the very ants assemble together and swarm over them. Those are the reasons which prove that the taste of flesh-meat must be exceedingly pleasant."

The king, hearing her argument, was pleased, and said, "Yes, daughter, meat is very pleasant as food. Everyone likes it." And he sent her away with a handsome present.

The second girl was then introduced, and of her the king inquired likewise, "What were you talking about last night under the tree?"

"I said nothing about you, O king," answered she.

"That is true, but what did you say?" asked the king.

"What I said," replied she, "was that there was no taste like the taste of wine."

"But whose daughter are you?" continued the king.

"I am," said she, "the daughter of a priest."

"A good joke, forsooth," said the king, smiling. "Priests hate the very name of wine. Then, what do you know of the taste of it?"

Then said the girl, "It is true I never touch wine, but I can easily understand how pleasant it is. I learn my lessons on the top of my father's house. Below are the wine shops. One day I saw two men nicely dressed, who came with their servants to buy wine at those shops, and there they sat and drank. After a time they got up and went away, but they staggered about from side to side, and I thought to myself, 'Here are these fellows rolling about, knocking themselves against the wall on this side, and falling against the wall on that. Surely they will never drink wine again!' However, I was mistaken, for the next day they came again and did the very same thing, and I considered, 'Wine must be very delicious to the taste, or else these persons would never have returned for more of it."

Then said the king, "Yes, O daughter, you are right. The taste of wine is very pleasant." And, giving her also a handsome present, he sent her home.

When the third girl entered the room, the king asked her in like manner, "O daughter, what were you talking about last night under the tree?"

"O king," answered she, "I made no reference to you."

"Quite so," said the king, "but tell me what it was you were saying."

"I was saying," replied she, "that there is no taste in the world so sweet as the taste of love-making."

"But," said the king, "you are a very young girl. What can you know about love-making? Whose daughter are you?"

"I am the daughter of a bard (a poet)," answered she. "It is true I am very young, but somehow I guess that love-making must be pleasant. My mother suffered so much when my little brother was born that she never expected to live. Yet, after a little time, she went back to her old ways and welcomed her lovers just the same as before. That is the reason I think that love-making must be so pleasant."

"What you say," observed the king, "cannot, O daughter, be justly denied." And he gave her a present equal in value to those of her friends and sent her, also, away.

When the fourth girl was introduced, the king put the same question to her, "Tell me what you and your companions talked about under the tree last night."

"It was not about the king," answered she.

"Nevertheless," asked he, "what was it you said?"

"Those who tell lies, said I, must tell them because they find the practice agreeable," replied she.

"Whose daughter are you?" inquired the king.

"I am the daughter of a farmer," answered the girl.

"And what made you think there was pleasure in telling lies?" asked the king.

The girl answered saucily, "Oh, you yourself will tell lies someday!"

"How?" said the king. "What can you mean?"

The girl answered, "If you will give me two lacs of rupees, and six months to consider, I will promise to prove my words."

So the king gave the girl the sum of money she asked for, and agreed to her conditions, sending her away with a present similar to those of the others.

After six months, he called her to his presence again, and reminded her of her promise. Now, in the interval the girl had built a fine palace far away in the forest, upon which she had expended the wealth which the king had given to her. It was beautifully adorned with carvings and paintings, and furnished with silk and satin. So she now said to the king, "Come with me, and you shall see God."

Taking with him two of his ministers, the king went out, and by the evening they all arrived at the palace.

"This palace is the abode of God," said the girl. "But he will reveal himself only to one person at a time, and he will not reveal himself even to him unless he was born in lawful wedlock. Therefore, while the rest remain without, let each of you enter in order."

"Be it so," said the king. "But let my ministers precede me. I shall go in last."

So the first minister passed through the door and at once found himself in a noble room, and as he looked around he said to himself, "Who knows whether I shall be permitted to see God or not? I may be base-born (born out of wedlock). And yet this place, so spacious and beautiful, is a fitting dwelling place even for the deity." With all his looking and straining, however, he quite failed to see God anywhere. Then said he to himself, "If now I go out and declare that I have not seen God, the king and the other minister will throw it in my teeth that I am base-born. I have one course open, therefore, which is to say that I have seen him."

So he went out, and when the king asked, "Have you seen God?" he answered at once, "Of course I have seen God."

"But have you really seen him?" continued the king.

"Really and truly," answered the minister.

"And what did he say to you?" inquired the king further.

"God commanded me not to divulge his words," readily answered the minister.

Then said the king to the other minister, "Now you go in."

The second minister lost no time in obeying his master's order, thinking in his heart as he crossed the threshold, "I wonder if I am base-born?" Finding himself in the midst of the magnificent chamber, he gazed about him on all sides, but failed to see God. Then said he to himself, "It is very possible I am base-born, for no God can I see. But it would be a lasting disgrace that I should admit it. I had better make out that I also have seen God."

Accordingly, he returned to the king, who said to him, "Well, have you seen God?" When the minister asserted that he had not only seen him, but that he had spoken with him too.

It was now the turn of the king, and he entered the room confident that he would be similarly favored. But he gazed around in dismay, perceiving no sign of anything which could even represent the Almighty. Then began he to think to himself, "This God, wherever he is, has been seen by both my ministers, and it cannot be denied, therefore, that their birthright is clear. Is it possible that I, the king, am base-born, seeing that no God appears to me? The very thought is confusion (an embarrassment), and necessity will compel me to assert that I have seen him too."

Having formed this resolution, the king stepped out and joined the rest of his party.

"And now, O king," asked the cunning girl, "have you also seen God?"

"Yes, answered he with assurance, "I have seen God."

"Really?" Asked she again.

"Certainly," asserted the king.

Three times the girl asked the same question, and three times the king unblushingly lied. Then said the girl, "O king, have you never a conscience? How could you possibly see God, seeing that God is a spirit?"

Hearing this reproof, the king recalled to mind the saying of the girl that one day he would lie too, and, with a laugh, he confessed that he had not seen God at all. The two ministers, beginning to feel alarmed, confessed the truth as well. Then said the girl, "O king, we poor people may tell lies occasionally to save our lives, but what had you to fear? Telling lies, therefore, for many has its own attractions, and to them at least the taste of lying is sweet."

Far from being offended at the stratagem (clever trick) which the girl had practiced on him, the king was so struck with her ingenuity and assurance that he married her forthwith, and in a short time she became his confidential adviser in all his affairs, public as well as private. Thus this simple girl came to great honor and renown, and so much did she grow in wisdom that her fame spread through many lands.[1]

Covering Up to Measure Up

"If now I go out and declare that I have not seen God, the king and the other minister will throw it in my teeth that I am base-born. I have only one course open, therefore, which is to say that I have seen him," said the first minister.

"It is very possible that I am base-born, for no God can I see. But it would be a lasting disgrace that I should admit it. I had better make out that I also have seen God," said the second minister.

"Is it possible that I, the king, am base-born, seeing that no God appears to me? The very thought is an embarrassment, and necessity will compel me to assert that I have seen him too," said the king.

The king and his two ministers are a lot like many of us. We can be content, comfortable, and confident until we begin basing our value and worth upon someone else's opinion of us. This may be because many of us really don't *know* who we are.

Who we are is our identity. What we do is our role. Out of our role, comes our image. Our downfall comes when we confuse our identity with our role. As a result, like the two ministers and the king, we will put on any pretenses we need to put on or tell any lie we need to tell in order to protect our role because we lack the knowledge and courage to stand unflinchingly flat-footed in our identity.

Even though our identity is who we are, we will use our role to define who we are in order to portray an image of whom we want people to believe we are. When we begin living according to our image, based upon our role, in negation of our identity, we relinquish our right to live according to our identity and thereby give to others the right to define us any way they so choose — and they will. This is a dangerous place to be because people then will become our gods.

Whether we realize it or not, or may be too prideful to admit, we all are born with the innate need to please. I believe it is a legitimate and unique feature placed within us by God to be used in conjunction with the gracious gifts and talents He has given to us all, to be used to bless others but even more, to please Him.

However, we have gotten it backwards and twisted. Many of us will use our talents and gifts to please and bless ourselves with material gain and to please people for emotional and promotional gain; so that in turn, they can put their stamp of approval on our worth and value; thereby giving to people a vaulted position in our lives they were never meant or equipped to occupy. Who among us can rightly determine the worth or value of another? Yet we continue to look to people for promotion based upon our role rather than to God based upon our identity.

When we relinquish our right to live according to our God-given identity, we willingly give people permission to redefine who we are rather than living based upon who we were created to become. As a result, we live without purpose and meaning and ultimately our lives become routinely and monotonously dull and unfulfilling because we are living outside of whom we really are while steadily striving to live according to what we believe others think we should be.

While there are as many reasons people lie as there are people, the motivations for lying are relatively few. The motivation for most lying is a desire either to hurt the one against whom the lie is directed (and we will discuss this in a later section) or to protect oneself, usually out of fear or pride.[2]

In our Western culture, role definition is viewed as key to who we are. I, perhaps like you, have the opportunity to meet a lot of people in both formal and casual settings. Almost without exception in the formal setting, the introductory exchange may go something like this, "Hi, I'm Liz, and I'm in marketing." To wit I will say, "Nice to meet you Liz, I'm Dorothy." If I don't immediately offer what I do as a qualifier of who I am, the next question out of Liz's mouth will likely be, "and Dorothy, what do you do?"

In a more casual setting the introductory exchange will go something like this, "Hi, I'm Liz."

"Nice meeting you Liz, my name is Dorothy."

Liz may go on about the weather, make comment on the event, the hostess, the host, the setting, but invariably, Liz will come back to, "and Dorothy, what do you do?"

The problems arise when we confuse who with what, and then magnifying the what exponentially for fear that who we are won't measure up to what we are expected to be. As a result, we find our sense of self and sense of significance in what we do rather than who we are, and we will fight to the death to hold on to what we do, because what we do defines who we are.

Let's look again at the two ministers and the king in our story. All three were the same three men that had left the king's palace before accompanying him on the journey with the young girl. They all were no doubt confident in whom they were, they had position and standing in the kingdom, and the king was top dog. Yet, at the mere suggestion that their worth and value would be predicated upon a condition the girl had made up, it changed their whole perspective and caused them to measure their worth based upon a statement of which they knew not the origin, from a person they had only met that day.

Given the same situation undoubtedly many of us would have done as the two ministers and king. In order to save face with their peers (pride), they each lied to cover up what they believed was a fatal flaw. Never mind it was a pseudo standard offered by a mere peasant, albeit clever girl. They willingly and eagerly believed and conformed to another's standard, giving up their own because each wanted so desperately to measure up in the eyes of their peers and boss based upon the same standard, no matter how flawed the standard may have been.

People, even well-meaning ones, make up all kinds of rules and legalisms. If we want to join their organization, party, group, or club; or, be viewed favorably by them, we will have to conform and be forced into the mold they pour for us — no matter how ill-fitting it may be. A square peg will never fit into a round hole.

Our God-given identity is a perfect fit for our God-given purpose, and we don't have to lie to please and impress others by attempting to fit into the restrictive and constrictive mold they take joy in pouring for us.

It all boils down to what and in whom we choose to believe. It is human nature for us to identify with something, some person, some movement, and some region of the country or part of the world. As a believer and follower of Jesus Christ, my identity is in Him — not in my job, my connections, my performance (good or bad) or the approval or disapproval of people. I have tried transcendentalism, my own brand of "isms" and was once an agnostic. In Christ, I have found peace in knowing that my identity is in Him and I am who He says I am — forgiven, redeemed, free of condemnation and that His love for me is unconditional. What a freeing and fun thing it is to no longer have to cover up to measure up. In Him, all I have to do is just be.

DANGEROUS IMPRESSIONS

"Love covers a multitude of sins" (1 Pet. 4:8) and lying can cover a multitude of tracks — but only for a while. It is often not the lie that causes our downfall, but the cover up. What tangled webs we all can weave but even the most practiced liars will eventually become ensnared in their tangled webs of deception.

A few years ago, there was a relatively young, seemingly affluent couple. Both were prominent in their own right, well known, well respected, and well liked. They seemed to have it all — wonderful friends, a nice home and were on the A-List of the movers and shakers. Both were politically active, politically savvy, fun to be around, always the life of the party, and were magnetically charming and graceful.

One weekday morning, the town was stunned as news of their murder-suicide hit the airwaves. The staggering reality of their deaths was devastating for family, friends, and colleagues. There was never a hint of trouble.

After the smoke cleared, it was evident from news reports that there were complicated and disturbing matters that had they lived, would have been difficult and embarrassing, though not impossible from which to recover.

Not long ago, I read a news story about a young professional man that had been recently laid off. He was ashamed to let his neighbors see him driving a Volvo because until the layoff he drove a Mercedes-Benz. Having to drive the Volvo was humiliating.

While these two real-life examples are extreme, together they make a point I want to get across. Whenever we lie to impress or to cover our tracks, we are setting ourselves up for an incredible fall. A cover up is a set up for failure and a cover up, once uncovered, will shatter even the most carefully crafted image.

We are more image-conscious today but less character-conscious. It seems to matter little anymore what we are on the inside, but more what we can portray ourselves to be on the outside. As a result, we spend countless hours at the gym, not necessarily to feel better, but to look better. And we spend billions of dollars on cosmetics and cosmetic surgery.

Over a matter of time however, after all of the things we've had sliced, diced and spiced begin to drip, drop and droop — again, we will be left with that which no amount of money can buy: our character. At the end of the day, it all comes down to something that doesn't cost a dime, character. A decaying character will eventually lead to a decayed image. And no amount of backtracking can ever change that, and may in fact make matters worse.

CAUGHT UP IN SOMEONE ELSE'S CRAZINESS

Many people fear what they don't understand, others will hate what they cannot have, and both will sometimes go to any length to destroy the one who has it.

Alternatively, others will see in someone else that which they abhor secretly about themselves. Consequently, they will turn self-hatred outward and will redirect it toward another or that which they represent, because it is a constant reminder of that which they so resent or fear in themselves. As a result, they will do whatever they can, as noticeably as they can, however they can, whenever they can, and garner the support of whomever they can, to destroy that person — even if it means lying to their recruited cohorts regarding the real reason they want to take him or her out. It has less to do with that person and more to do with what is going on inside of them. By annihilating the target of their hatred, they annihilate the threatening thing within them they so greatly loathe or long for — or so they think. But not so fast! Once they successfully destroy *that* person, there will be someone else of the same ilk that will become the object of their inside-out hatred. It never fails.

This is why it is dangerous to believe off-hand the worst about people based upon what we have heard from other people. It is important we not take at face value the derogatory and disparaging things said by others about others and make snap judgments based upon what we have heard rather than what we have discovered on our own to be true.

Find the facts before finding fault. Moreover, pay close attention to who and what people rail most vehemently against and fight the temptation to allow yourself without legitimate reason to be sucked into their craziness. Unknown to you, they quite possibly could be guilty of the same; are the same; want desperately to be the same; fear becoming the same or even worse, fear someone will find out they have done or are doing the same. We can never be certain of anyone's motives because motives are hatched in the mind and are harbored in the heart. None of us is equipped with x-ray vision to peer into either.

People are not always what they appear and neither are their motives. Since we can't read minds or examine the inner workings of another's heart, I have learned to ask God for discernment regarding anyone with whom I find myself spending any length of time — personally and professionally. I have also learned to talk less but listen and observe more. If you listen and observe closely enough, people will invariably reveal who they are. Once you know who they are, it won't take very long to figure out what they are about — without exception. Consequently, you will be less likely to take on anger that isn't yours, issues that aren't yours, and baggage you were never meant or equipped to carry. "Be quick to hear, slow to speak *and* slow to anger" (James 1:19).

Learning the skills of active listening and quiet observation can be two of the greatest assets you could ever acquire. You can never distinguish a lie from the truth if you're always the one doing all the talking. If you have the opportunity to be in the presence of a dynamic leader, take note. While he or she may be the most powerful one in the meeting, they often are the most quiet, not because they are disinterested or daydreaming. They are making observations, while carefully reading the situation in order to make the most strategic decision.

You learn more about people, situations, and motives by speaking less and listening more. With practice, anyone can learn these skills without having to spend a dime on expensive seminars. Practice is free.

Sometimes our greatest downfall isn't a result of what we do, but a result of with whom we choose to associate and whom we choose to follow. If not careful, we could be led right off the cliff by following those we think we know, based upon information we did not know. Without the wisdom of discernment, we can't even be sure when and if people are using us in order to position us to fail. While we may have been led to believe we are joining them in the pursuit of someone else, we ourselves may be their targeted game.

Since many of us can't turn away from hearing juicy bits of gossip, we can so easily but erroneously base our opinions and actions upon what we hear rather than what we know; taking as gospel what people say without taking into consideration the possibility that we could be used in their vengeful game of revenge. Even more, we could be setting ourselves up unsuspectingly for a fall — one we will never see coming.

When we go along with sinister schemes, plots and plans designed to bring intentional harm, and gleefully join in digging a pit from which we're certain the person will never climb, we're setting ourselves up for a dangerous fall. The same pit we hollow out for someone else will become the same pit into which we will eventually fall (see Psalm 7:15).

If you have been in a pit for a while, and no matter what you do you can't regain your footing, think back for a minute or two. Perhaps you are in the pit today that you grabbed a shovel for yesterday to dig or help dig for someone else. That's not an easy one to admit, but I can't stress enough how true it is. Maybe it is time to make a phone call, send an e-mail, or pay a visit to make amends. At this point, what more do you have left to lose?

A WORD TO THE WISE ABOUT LIES

Mark Twain said, "A lie can travel halfway around the world while the truth is still putting on its shoes." What was true a century ago is still true today except in our instantaneous, 24/7 news cycle world, a lie can travel throughout the world in a matter of nanoseconds. Even more, lies grow feet. When they do, they will chase us down and stomp our reputation, relationships, and career into the ground.

I realize that lying is, always has been, and always will be part of the fabric of our humanity; and that some may blow all of this off and will keep lying as they have always lied, and will keep lining up behind those who lie for sport.

After all, if lying has worked so well up until now, why bother to change? So what if we lie every now and then to cover our tracks, get our way, or to shove someone out of the way — no harm, no foul, right? Wrong. A liar will not go unpunished and there is no escape for those who lie (Prov. 19:5; author paraphrase). This is a universal truth. What is covered will be uncovered and a lie meant for the destruction of another will ultimately cause the destruction of the one who sought to destroy.

Lies are birthed with strings and come with price tags. As a lie grows and spins out of control, the strings will unravel and the price tag will increase. Since none of us live in isolation, someone somewhere will likely know our truth. When we are finally forced to come clean, the price tag will be steep — costing us our marriage, ministry, career, or reputation.

Whoever knows our truth can pull our strings. Don't give that power to anyone. Admit the truth before you feel the first tug of the string. Otherwise, you may be in for an embarrassing and humiliating fall.

Lies are cheap but their price tag can be steep. Truth in this digital age, sooner or later will be discovered and often at a pivotal point in our life or career when the potential is highest to do the most damage.

We all struggle in various ways with various issues. There are no perfect people. I am no exception. You are no exception. Some of the things you and I have done are thankfully known only by God and we will take them to our grave. However, one thing is certain. If we don't face head-on and deal forthrightly with our issues, our issues invariably will deal unmercifully with us. In continuing to cover our tracks with lies, we will take outrageous risks or make foolish mistakes in judgment which will lead to our downfall. And the higher up the food chain we climb, the greater the feeding frenzy when we fall.

Destructive tendencies or issues we have long fought to ignore, have secretly engaged in or have suppressed for years, have a way of bubbling to the top at the most inopportune time. When they do, they will cause a stunning and humiliating fall. The surprising downfall of many we hold in high esteem can often be traced directly back to a refusal to deal with distasteful, often deep-seated issues. Money can't fix this. Positions of influence can't fix this. They can only camouflage, but never cure. The only cure for a lie is the truth — and it begins with taking our own medicine by being true to ourselves.

If you don't get anything else from this chapter, please get this. Not speaking from what I have learned in a classroom or by reading a book, but from what I have learned from my own life — the most venomous lies are not those others tell about us, though they can be brutal, but the worst are those we tell ourselves about ourselves. I have no way of knowing if this applies to you, but if it does, I want to share with you the same sobering but liberating advice I one day looked squarely into the mirror and shared with myself. As delicately as I can put this, stop lying to yourself. Deal with your demons and defeat them now so they won't deal with and defeat you later.

Our capacity to cause damage to ourselves far outweighs the ability of others to do the same. Don't be afraid to face your issues, particularly those that run counter to who and what you hold yourself out to be; because those will be the very ones that will cause your most agonizing fall and wreck your credibility.

A hypocrite is like the little boy that cried wolf. Once it is proven that everything you claim to stand for is a lie, people may never trust you again; and the authority from which you spoke will be painfully snatched away. You will be left with nothing.

Those secret sins, secret addictions, enticing tendencies, strongholds, moral or ethical challenges, masked but true beliefs, even feigning affection we no longer have for our spouse or significant other, are the kinds of things that if not confessed and dealt with, will invariably lead to some measure of loss; and a numbing fall from grace because we will eventually seek ways to satisfy our secrets.

Admittedly, it is impossible for any of us to be 100% truthful 100% of the time because we all are 100% human — no excuse, just a fact. Nevertheless, we should make it a practice to be honest, particularly with ourselves.

Who are you, really? Only by knowing your true identity will you be able to flourish in who you were meant to be. Otherwise, you will fail in who you are trying to be.

If we refuse to be honest with ourselves, we won't be honest with anyone else.

If a man could second guess his mistakes, he'd never die by accident.

– Michael Landon as Little Joe Cartwright
from the Bonanza series episode, "Credit for a Kill,"
National Broadcasting Company (NBC), 1966.

I was a risk taker,

a mover and a shaker.

I didn't mind rolling the dice,

Everything I touched turned out nice.

I had money, women, influence and cars.

No one could have told me I'd be behind bars.

I played the fool and threw it all away.

I guess they were right, every dog has his day.

CHAPTER 5

∽

UNDERESTIMATING RISKS: RISK V. REWARD

"There is a way which seems right to a man, But its end is the way of death."

Proverbs 14:12

Anyone with the tenacity to succeed is a risk taker. There can be neither victory nor success without taking risks. While risk-taking is commendable, risqué behavior is stupid. Who we are determines what we will do and sometimes we don't discover who we truly are until we get caught up in things we thought we'd never do with people with whom we thought we never would. I am not saying that makes us stupid. What I am saying, however, is by not knowing who we are, and not knowing our limitations can cause us to do some outrageously stupid things. Dirty Harry was right, "A man's got to know his limitations." I might add, so do women.

When we underestimate risks, it is not that we don't know better. We just lose sight of who we are, what we represent, and foolishly deceive ourselves into thinking that we can get by with it. Hamstrung by emotion or trapped by greed, we simply don't stop to consider the consequential costs of getting caught.

Talented risk takers have three things in common — passion, perseverance, and the propensity to believe we can handle anything that comes our way. Great traits. However, we can't be hard-boiled risk takers with poached egg character because our talents will take us where our character can't keep us. Even more, the same robust passion that drives us to take risks is the same robust passion that can drive us over the edge.

THE ENEMY IN YOU AND THE ENEMY IN ME

Corruption and sex scandals pepper newscasts and the Internet. It is not only the high-profile stars, politicians, preachers, and athletes, but also everyday working people who are being stung by stings that are as sad as they are salacious.

"We have met the enemy and he is us," said the fictional cartoon character, Pogo. The enemy in you and the enemy in me is one that causes good people to do bad things, intelligent people to make less than intelligent choices, and, moral people to dive headlong into the cesspool of immorality.

Many have been held fast by its grip, as it lurks silently undetected within us all, waiting for the right opportunity and the right time to seize our hearts and engulf our minds to the point that it takes over our thoughts, feelings, and our very actions. We all have it, we are born with it, it grows as we grow, moves when we move, and it feeds off the desires inherent to us all — the desire for sex, the desire for stuff (material things) and the desire for status. It is lust.

If a weakness borne out of these three (sex, stuff or status) becomes evident to it, and at the same time an object of one of these three becomes available for it, it begins rising up in anticipation of springing into action. And when it grips our heart and engulfs our mind, it will push us and drive us to make choices and take risks that may prove in the end lethal. This self-gratification at the expense of all else can cause us to lose our careers, marriages, and reputations.

When timing, opportunity, and our weakness line up, we will find ourselves in a wrestling match with this enemy for which we are no match, and one we rarely ever see coming. We can fight an enemy we can see, but it is difficult to fight one we can only feel — made even more difficult because it feels so good. Everyone will have to tussle on some level, at some point in their lives, with this enemy.

That is why it is dangerous to look down on or point fingers at anyone who seemed to have thrown caution to the wind and did something that to us may have seemed incredibly idiotic that cost them their marriage or career. Conversely, it is just as dangerous to put people on pedestals, thinking, given their status, they would never, could never do anything so hideous as to have an affair, take a bribe, or embezzle money from their company. When caught in the lustful grip of self-gratification, all of us are capable of doing anything, at any time, given the right opportunity.

Will power is no match for the power of lust. Lust is a sin which makes it a spiritual enemy and we can't fight a spiritual enemy with a psychological weapon. More definitively, lust is a desire for that which is contrary to the will of God. Therefore, it is going to take the power of God's word and not the puniness of our will to overcome it.

We will never experience the brunt of its full power until we find ourselves overtaken by its seductive lure as it takes us to places we don't want to go and to which we swear we will never return — until we find ourselves there again and again, staying when we know we should go and saying yes when we know we should say no. The pull of sex, the craving for money, status, and material things can be overpowering. As much as we don't want to give in, we find ourselves helplessly giving in to the guilty pleasure of satisfying an enemy we seem powerless to defeat. The Apostle Paul verbalized beautifully this feeling of helplessness in Romans 7:15-19:

"For what I am doing, I do not understand; for I am not practicing what I *would* like to *do*, but I am doing the very thing I hate...So now, no longer am I the one doing it, but sin which dwells in me. For I know that nothing good dwells in me, that is, in my flesh; for the willing is present in me, but the doing of the good *is* not. For the good that I want, I do not do, but I practice the very evil that I do not want."

Before moving on, let me share with you a little of the background of the man who so eloquently wrote centuries ago what many of us are going through right now. Paul came from a well-to-do family, was highly educated, had credentials galore and was a charismatic leader. Why do I include this? Because some of us have the erroneous, sanctimonious idea that given our background, education, church membership, or standing in the community, we are somehow better than others and can't possibly take senseless risks and become ensnared in distasteful situations. That is far from true. Lust has bait for everybody. What hooks me may not hook you. Nevertheless, we all have a worm or a lure waiting at the end of a hook — somewhere. Before we jump and take the bait, take the risk, we should ask ourselves these key questions. If I take this risk:

Will it hurt someone I love or care about
if they found out?
Could it damage my name, reputation,
or credibility if it were made public?
Can it cost me my career?
Would I be embarrassed if it were broadcast
on the local news?

If the answer is yes to any one of these it is a high risk with zero return. If you take it, you may be sorry you did.

THE BIG THREE

It is always amusing to listen to interviews of people who through friendship or kinship know someone who recently committed a horrible act or got busted in a sting operation which led to their swift and scandalous fall. People will invariably say things such as, "No one would have ever guessed he was on the take." Or, "There was never any indication she would do such a thing." Or, "They looked like the perfect couple; none of us ever saw this coming."

Lust can't be seen, only exemplified through our actions. It is an intensely private desire manifested publicly by what and how much we are willing to risk satisfying it. When we take a personal risk to satisfy a private passion, it will have its genesis in one of these three: (paraphrased from 1 John 2:15-16)

- Sex (lust of the flesh)

- Stuff (lust of the eyes)

- Status (boastful pride of life)

These have been, are, and will be the reasons behind the most stunning falls. No one is above them and without empowerment from on high; even the most esteemed, respected, successful, intelligent, faithful pillars of your community and mine cannot escape risking it all for them. "Good" people whom no one would ever suspect would do "bad" things are not exempt or immune. On the contrary, they sometimes are more likely because it is so easy to hide behind their perceived goodness. We can sometimes believe we can skate beneath the radar of bad behavior because we have proven how "good and godly" we are. Don't be fooled. It is a bad thing to get caught up in our own goodness.

However, good people are good at hiding fatal flaws. Those who are masters at putting on fronts in public are nothing but amateurs in the final analysis as they clumsily stumble through passionate denials of a dreadful mistake. With a roll of the dice, some have lost positions of prominence they can never recapture and have damaged relationships they can never repair because they failed to weigh the risks against the rewards.

The big three have hooked big and small fish, with embarrassing results causing astonishing downfalls. For some it was the public breakup of a marriage, for others the abrupt end of a promising career, still tragically for others the loss of a sterling reputation. Things such as corruption, or a fling at the office, have thrown a wrench into the lives of countless of people bringing to a screeching halt life as they knew it before a foolhardy self-centered, ill-advised risk caused them to lose it all.

Sex, the craving for more "stuff" and a preoccupation with status have brought to their knees some of the most powerful, influential, and leading business, political, religious and community leaders of our time. I would even dare say of all time. More important for you and me, they just as easily could do the same to us.

SEX — LUST OF THE FLESH

Sex scandals have rocked the airwaves to the point where we have become desensitized to the sensational. Instantaneous and prolific news fulfills our voyeuristic need to peek into the private lives of others. Anyone with a cell phone is now part of the paparazzi. What once was the worry of public figures should be a concern to us all because individual privacy is quickly giving way to the public's right to know. What once was private can now instantly become public, secret sex is far less secretive, and in today's world, can have devastatingly public results.

Risking it all in the name of love or for the sake of sexual satisfaction is nothing new, but no less dangerous. We have become more reckless, more ruthless, and as a result, we are living in a culture that has become morally bankrupt and struggling to find its way. Those who dare say differently are ridiculed as prudes, homophobes, haters, or Jesus freaks. I am none of these. However, the proliferation of sexually transmitted diseases in younger and younger age groups, the trail of broken dreams from broken homes — broken up by a casual sexual encounter or affair — should cause us all some degree of consternation.

The risks of putting our marriage and family on the line for the sake of outside sex are incalculable. This is the one risk where each answer to the four previous questions would be yes with a capital "Y" which is a real good indication that this risk is always, always a bad one to take. Why? Because marriage is not just cake and punch, a honeymoon, house and kids. It is a covenant. In fact, it is the only covenant of permanency we make before God. But if God means nothing to us, the word "covenant" will mean nothing to us. And since that word will mean nothing to us, then it follows that our marriage will mean nothing to us. It isn't a matter of how much or how little we love our husband or wife — it is a matter of how much we revere God.

Those of us who have spent any amount of time in church or have listened to stories from the Bible may remember well the story of Joseph and Potiphar's wife (see Genesis 39:7-20). Joseph was Potiphar's personal servant. Potiphar put Joseph in charge of not only his entire household, but all that he owned. Joseph was successful and handsome. One day, Potiphar's wife attempted to seduce him. It would have been an easy thing for Joseph to do, but he refused. He exhibited moral character in that he refused to sleep with her based upon his loyalty to Potiphar and in appreciation of the trust and confidence Potiphar had placed in him. Moreover, Joseph understood the gravity of marriage and its covenant. In rebuffing her he said, "There is no one greater in this house than I, and he (Potiphar) has withheld nothing from me except you, because you are his wife. **How then could I do this great evil and sin against God?"** (Gen. 39:9; author emphasis).

For some of us, adultery has become no big deal because God has become no big deal. We no longer fear breaking our covenant because we no longer fear disobeying God's word. When we choose to cheat, we are not just cheating on our spouses; we are also cheating on God because marriage is a tripartite covenant between you, your spouse, and God. That is why the price we pay for infidelity is so steep — not just monetarily, but also the horrendous, exponential emotional and psychological toll it takes on the three parties, their families, friends, and others who care about them.

Why am I spending so much time explaining this? Because just like with lying, if we don't understand the spiritual underpinning of the physical things we do, and how the pieces of the puzzle fit, we will continue to fall and fail and miss out on the best life has to offer. We will underestimate the risks because we will continue to base them on how we feel, rather than what is real.

Even though many couples today are cleverly and intentionally leaving out any "religious" references in their marriage ceremonies, it does not negate the fact that marriage is a covenantal act. Two people, a man and a woman, become one. It doesn't matter if we choose to ignore the spiritual significance of that or not. We can ignore a STOP sign and blow right through it without recognizing its significance. That does not negate the fact that the STOP sign is there.

In the breakup of a marriage caused by infidelity, something always dies, beginning with trust. Not only will it be difficult to regain the trust of your family, but perhaps even your boss. If you cheat on your spouse, what is to keep your boss from doubting you will cheat on your expense account or time sheet?

The affair at the office may end, but there could be lingering consequences that will overshadow your career and life for years to come. You may be passed over for the promotion you were a sure bet to get, or you may get transferred to the department from hell; or worse, forced into retirement sooner than you had anticipated. There could be a sudden or debilitating illness that hinders you or your spouse from working or working full-time and you fall into financial ruin. There could be a number of seemingly disjointed events that happen, and we will never stop to put two and two together.

There is always a penalty to pay for infidelity — always. Does God forgive? Yes, He does; however, there will still be consequences. Equally frightening is the possibility of generational consequences. The consequences of infidelity may not occur until the next generation or perhaps even subsequent ones because a parent's sin can negatively impact the lives of his or her children, grandchildren, or great-grandchildren. This is no arbitrary punishment and you in fact could today be suffering the consequences of unrepentant moral failure or other unrepentant transgressions committed by your parents, grandparents, or great-grandparents long before you were even a thought.

The risks associated with an unrepentant sexual relationship outside of marriage may seem minimal at first and the thrilling, clandestine meetings and spine tingling kisses rejuvenating, exhilarating, and fun — but only for a while. There always will be a steep price to pay. The kicker is, we never know just what the price will be and how much and how long we will end up paying. If you ever get around to counting the costs, don't exclude the X-factor — the consequences. They can be devastating not only for you, but also possibly for your children, grandchildren, all the way down to the fourth generation (see Exodus 34:7). Think about that the next time you're lying in bed with your mistress or lover. Getting caught should be the least of your worries.

KNOWING OUR LIMITATIONS

If we would take time for reflection and introspection in order to become better acquainted with ourselves and more importantly our limitations, we wouldn't take the wanton risks that we sometimes take that invariably can lead to a startling downfall. As I mentioned earlier, never say what you won't do and never underestimate what people *will* do. No matter how successful, wealthy, popular, religious, well respected, intelligent, and blue-blooded a person may be, appearances are deceiving. Pedigree, popularity, and pomposity are poor indicators of purity. No one has clean hands — no one. That is why it is dangerous to point out the dirty hands of someone else, when we haven't examined our own palms.

I suggest that as often as you can, be your own lunch or dinner date, even if you're married — especially if you are married. We can lose ourselves in our relationships and if not careful, lose ourselves in the process. Make a dinner date with yourself, if it is nowhere but to McDonald's® and have a nice, quiet introspective dinner conversation. At least twice a year, get away for the weekend — with you. I know some may think this is selfish, bordering on extreme. However, think of all the time you spend on your job, learning the likes and dislikes of your boss, time spent getting to know other people, time spent with your kids, tending to elderly parents, in class, surfing the Net, serving in organizations, on various boards in your church or community. Then think of the amount of time you spend with just you.

Why is it important? We change. Nothing profound — over time we simply change and so do our needs. However, because we are so busy, we are sometimes unaware of the ways in which our needs and we have changed — even more important, *how* our needs have changed. For example, I don't need the same things today from my husband that I needed from him ten years ago, nor he from me. We all change. Our relationships change, our children change, our desires, expectations, and goals change.

When we find ourselves doing things we thought we'd never do with someone with whom we thought we never would — and beating ourselves up for it — it is because psychologically we are relating to ourselves as we have always known ourselves, without realizing that emotionally and mentally, we have changed and more important, that our needs have changed. We rarely stop to consider the ways in which our emotional and spiritual needs have changed. As a result, we sometimes walk around in a funk, not realizing why. We think something is "wrong" when externally everything is "right" because we can't verbalize what we don't understand. If you're a husband and this describes your wife, she is probably driving you nuts, or vice versa.

We beat ourselves up without realizing that the person we are beating up is the person whom we knew ourselves to be in times past, who we still believe ourselves to be, without realizing in a very real way, we aren't. You consistently ask yourself the question, "What is wrong with me?" Or say to yourself, "This is not who I am." You're wrong. It is who you are *today*. The problem is many of us are still stuck in yesterday's mentality.

The person you are relating to was the person you were two years ago, maybe even ten years ago, etc., and in that, you are right; because that person *wouldn't* be doing what you are doing today. But you have changed! You have just been too busy to notice. When we find ourselves doing things we thought we'd never do, it is because we are acting consciously on an unconscious need we likely never realized we had.

It is sometimes heart wrenching counseling tortured people on both sides of an affair because hurting and disappointing their family is the last thing they would have ever wanted to do. Some often say how much they wanted to stop, but couldn't. It is largely because the other person filled an unmet perhaps even unconscious need. The fulfillment of that need became intoxicating, rejuvenating, and in a way almost addictive — so much so that they were willing to put at risk everything for which they had worked: their reputation, marriage, credibility, and career. Sometimes, these relationships aren't merely about sex, but more for the fulfillment of an emotional need. Are you up to speed on your needs? If not, you're vulnerable and

Satan never misses an opportunity to take advantage of our vulnerabilities.

Spending time alone is a necessity because it is only through the tranquility of reflection, introspection, and revelation that we come to grips with our needs, what drives us, what moves us, what turns us on, what turns us off, what pushes our buttons, where we are most vulnerable, etc. It is during the stillness of these moments when we should ask God to reveal to us, us. He will gladly oblige, often to our chagrin. I suggest beginning the conversation with Psalm 139:23:

"Search me, O God, and know my heart; Try me and know my anxious thoughts; And see if there be any hurtful way in me, And lead me in the everlasting way."

You are asking God to perform a spiritual MRI to reveal harmful thought patterns and rotten areas of the heart that could damage, harm and negatively influence you; and, to lead you in the right way — His way. Why is this important?

Every action we take begins with a thought. Our thoughts are filtered through our heart. As a result, the words that come out of our mouth and the ways in which we respond, originate in our head, but emanate from our heart (see Proverbs 4:23; Luke 6:45).

Whatever or whomever controls our head controls our heart, and will control our actions. If our thinking is wrong, how we feel about what we are thinking will be wrong; therefore, the way in which we respond to what we are feeling, based upon what we're thinking, will be wrong.

If we don't know ourselves well enough to know if it is God who is controlling our head and ultimately our heart and actions, or if it is Satan controlling our head and ultimately our heart and actions, we are in serious, deep trouble. The only way others and we will know will be through how we respond and react. For those who don't share the Christian faith, let me put it this way. You can talk a good game all day long, but it's how you perform on the field that counts. Actions speak louder than words.

For years, practically all of my life, I didn't understand this principle of the head and the heart. To be honest, I had no idea who I was, what my limitations are, and it cost me, more than once, more than twice. Today, I can thankfully say that is not the case. As a result of regular spiritual MRIs and getting to better know me and better understand me, I am a much better wife, mother, sister, friend, servant, and person. I am still far from perfect, but at least now I know what and where the imperfections are — the rest is a piece of cake.

Getting to know who we *really* are can be a scary undertaking. It is like that long overdue checkup appointment with the doctor we know we should have made years ago, but keep putting off because we are afraid of what he or she may find. However, not knowing could prove dangerous, if not fatal. It is the same principle at play here. We *think* we're okay; however, if we're not, we don't want to know.

Unless we understand and know our limitations, invariably a situation will arise that will push our buttons. We will react in a way that will not only surprise and disappoint others but also ourselves. Our overreaction could damage our reputation, career, credibility; and, far more damaging for believers, our witness for Christ.

The better we know ourselves, the better we can control ourselves and the less we will be controlled by our emotions, other people's opinions, their like or dislike of us. Victory lies with those who can maintain composure and self-control. However, you cannot control that of which you have no knowledge. If you don't know yourself, you will not be able to control yourself. Philosopher Lao-Tzu put it thusly, "He who controls others may be powerful, but he who has mastered himself is mightier still."

I don't know about you, but I would rather be a master of the game than the best player on the court.

We all need preventative mental and emotional maintenance. We spend more time getting our cars tuned than we do getting our head and heart tuned. Isn't it about time you scheduled that MRI with God?

LOVE OR LUST — YOU DECIDE

You recently met this wonderful man or woman, and you are convinced it was love at first sight. Stolen kisses, knowing glances across the room, long romantic dinners, and long walks in the park all feel so right. You love everything about them, from the way they dress to the way they smell — especially the way they smell. The sweet, light fragrance of her perfume or the earthy, clean scent of his cologne sends you into orbit. You can't get enough of being with them and when apart, penetrating thoughts of them occupy your mind and keep you going until you can be together again.

You think about them at work as you try concentrating during meetings, yet like a school kid with a serious crush, you can't help but scribble their name when you should be scribbling meeting notes. You think of them at the gym as you're working out and can't help but put in the extra effort because you want them to notice. When you shop, you select clothes you think they'd like and those that accentuate your best features. The cell phone is always on — you would kick yourself if you missed their call because the sound of their voice takes your breath away. You can't believe how deeply you both have fallen in love in such a short time and you can't wait to spend the rest of your life together.

Love and lust so mimic one another that if we miss or minimize the subtle differences, we could make a mistake that could forever alter the course of our life — and not for the better. You may think you have fallen in love when actually you have been overcome by lust. So, how *can* you tell?

Love	Lust
Patient	Impatient; Can't wait to...
Considerate	Selfish
Other person's needs come first	My needs come first
When gratified grows	When gratified fizzles
Trusting	Jealous
Reserved	Brags
Humble	Full of yourself
Understanding	Demanding
Forgiving	Unforgiving
Supportive	Self-centered
In for the long haul	Stays as long as needs are met
Spiritual/Emotional/Physical Balance	Physical

The magnetic draw of the physical, aphrodisiacal distinctiveness of another is undeniably powerful. However, the key word here is *physical*. It will feel so good — but only for so long.

The distinguishing clue is that lust once satisfied can quickly dissolve into indifference, boredom or even hatred. The searing, intense passion that burned so hotly can hastily turn harsh. Like a weed, lust grows quickly but has no root system. It becomes one-dimensional and shallow, and sex will serve as both the foundation to hold it up and the scaffolding to hold it together. With lust, the relationship becomes more complicated and less fun; with love, the relationship becomes more fun and less complicated. At times without explanation, lust can turn cold and distant and the "you and me against the world" and "the all about us" can turn to disgust as you begin to turn on one another. When passion wanes, not only do you become disgusted with them but also yourself. This can lead to depression, a repetitive cycle of aggression that you will loathe but can't seem to stop as you try desperately to recreate that amazing experience, only to be left with remorse and recurring emptiness.

Lust of the flesh can take you to the moon and over the rainbow. However, don't be surprised if instead of a pot of gold at the end, there is only a pot of shame. You will be left not only empty and ashamed. If married, you would have broken your vows, trashed your covenant, and where there once was life, there will be death — chief among them death of trust and self-respect. Lust can excite but it can't resuscitate that part of you that dies when you trust it with your heart. It takes, but never gives; destroys, but never builds. Capable of only satisfying itself, once satisfied, it leaves you alone to pick up the pieces of what will be your shattered and broken life. Count the costs.

Love or lust?
When in doubt, don't.
Love will wait,
but lust just won't.

Stuff — Lust of the Eyes

He was a 47-year-old highly successful, well traveled, well connected, multi-millionaire. He shared a magnificent five-storey home with his beautiful wife and eight-year-old son. Life had been good. One morning as was his custom, he kissed his wife goodbye as he dashed out of the door heading for the office.

About an hour later, he e-mailed her to discuss plans for a weekend getaway. Not less than 20 minutes later, he leaped from the platform of an intercity rail station into the path of an oncoming train that was bearing down at 125 mph. As he bravely turned to meet head-on his doom, the train smashed into him, killing him instantly — true story.

What would make a young, well-educated, wealthy, devoted husband and father choose to end it all in such a gruesome way? The answer came days later from his still shocked and grieving wife. She explained that he was facing serious financial loss and feared financial ruin. However, there was no indication it was bad enough to make him take his own life.

Whenever our sense of worth becomes an essential part of the bottom line of our net worth, when our net worth diminishes, so will our sense of self-worth. If we don't have a foundation rooted in something other than what we perceive is our net worth, based upon the net worth of our bank account, we are going to bottom out fairly quickly because money and material things are never permanent — and were never meant to determine who and what we are. Besides, one day, we all are going to leave it all behind.

For those hooked by the burning desire to obtain more — more money, more cars, more clothes, more stuff — your need isn't so much about the money and stuff, but about these four areas of human existence:

- Power

- Influence

- Control

- Success

It is not so much the *stuff* you crave; it is what the stuff affords you.

POWER

For some, the lust for material things and money can be directly tied to their lust for power. The more money they have and the more symbols of wealth they can accumulate, the more powerful they will become in their minds and in the eyes of people.

Money gives us the power to say yes and the freedom to say no. It comes with the assurance of knowing you can take people or leave them, walk away or stay. Power puts you in the catbird seat and in the driver's seat. Nothing happens without your blessing, and nobody isn't anybody until *you* say they're somebody.

Those who lust for money and material things out of a need for power see money and material things as the means to that end. Some could care less about the money. But without the money, there would be no power. You would be surprised at the number of powerful people who find less joy in spending money and more joy in accumulating money. It is the accumulation of wealth that gives them their sense of power.

If not careful, however, your love for power will replace your love for God. When that happens, you're in for a fall because the very first commandment is that we have no other gods before Him (see Exodus 20:3). If, through the lust for money, you obtain the power that you seek, don't forget the source of the power. It isn't your money. The day you begin to believe you have what you have because of your ingenuity or financial acumen — mark that date on your calendar, because it will be the first day of the beginning of your downfall.

It is God who gives us the ability to make wealth (see Deuteronomy 8:18) and the moment we forget that is the moment when our power will begin to wane and erode. It may not be noticeable right away and it may be gradual and slow. Or, as in the case of the swift and severe meltdown of the worldwide markets we are still experiencing, it could literally happen overnight. Don't force a power play with the All Powerful — you will lose every time.

INFLUENCE

Others are not driven by the overarching need for power, but by the burning desire to have the ability to influence circumstances, outcomes, and hold sway over programs, people, and livelihoods. People of influence may not be and in most cases are not, the people with the ultimate power, but merely the people with the influence who have access to the people with power; or, are in a position to influence outcomes to their advantage or favor. They have a deep need for acceptance and work hard to gain and maintain that acceptance through relationships and the accumulation of money and material things.

Driving the right car, wearing the right clothes, belonging to the right country club or civic organization is extremely important. Whereas the person driven by the need for power cares more about the power than the money, the person driven by the need to influence cares more about the money than the power. They don't at all mind going into debt to maintain the lifestyle necessary to allow them to remain in the inner circle and on the A-List of the powerful.

Those driven by influence enjoy well their roles as gate-keeper. It gives them a sense of importance, and to a lesser degree, power, to have the ability to be the one to say yay or nay to requests, or yay or nay to access to the person for whom they hold the door. In this case, you would at times think they are more important than the person for whom they serve as front man or woman. Even more, as strange as it may seem, you would think the one driven by power would want people to bow down and kiss their ring. Most of the time that is not the case — it is the one driven by influence who wants people to take that bow.

A word of warning to the one whom this describes, be careful. The very people whom you are seeking to serve as the access point for will be the same people who will boot you when you become a liability. You will become a liability when you begin to believe that you are "the man" or "the woman" instead of the powerful person for whom you serve as gatekeeper.

Just like God will have no other god before Him, even though it may not be evident on the outside, a number of pow-erful people suffer from the god complex. They too will have no other god before them. And if they sense you think that you have now somehow arrived to the point that you are on their level, their natural inclination is to show you that you haven't and to show you the door.

Secondly, because you hold the livelihoods of people in your hands, the temptation will be to squeeze as much as you can out of them since they have to come through you in order to meet their goal or objective. Quid pro quo however can be a dangerous proposition especially for politicians and public servants. Influence is a breeding ground for corruption and it is all too easy for the influencer to become the influenced.

Be thankful for the position you hold, practice humility, and be kind to people who need your help. Don't require or expect people to kiss your ring, because there may come a time when the script is flipped and you may be the one having to bow.

CONTROL

For those who have a strong need to control, their lust for money and material things is not for the sake of power or influence, but for the need to exercise control over people and manipulate circumstances to their advantage. Their lust for money and stuff is to allow them to have complete control over those who are dependent upon them. Most of the time, it is close family members or employees.

Controllers have low self-esteem and if their weakness is money, they find their esteem in money and possessions only because of the opportunity it affords them to use one or both to manipulate and control others. Again, the lust for money and things is only a means of satisfying a deeper need; and in the case of controllers, it is the need to control and manipulate.

The very thing that drives them to pursue more money and more material things will be the same thing that drives their downfall. There will come a day when there will be a circumstance they have absolutely no control to influence, manipulate, or change. That is by design. Controllers lose sight of the fact that they really aren't in control at all. God is. And if it takes showing them, He will by arranging circumstances in a way that no amount of money could change.

So, to the one who lusts after money and material things because of the ability it affords you to control and manipulate, be careful. God has a way of letting us know who is *really* in control.

SUCCESS

For most of us, the lust for money and material things is not about power, influence or control — while certainly those things are elements, our lust for money and stuff is less complicated. We simply want to prove we are successful. No one is successful unless they have something to show they are successful; hence, the desire to live in certain neighborhoods, drive certain cars and even more important, to be viewed by others as having "made it."

We steadily climb the ladder of success with our eyes always on the corner office. A testament to our success is a great career, great family, discretionary income, the ability to travel, and the ability to give philanthropically. There is nothing wrong with wanting to succeed, working to succeed, and enjoying the fruit of your labor as a result of succeeding.

However, the problem with those who are driven to accumulate money and material things in the name of success is they can easily become overly ambitious in their drive to do so. We all need ambition and ambition is a good thing. But when we become blinded by ambition in our quest to become successful, we are treading on thin ice. As ambitions and successes grow, so can our ego. When ego takes over our desire for money and material things for the sake of ego rather than for the sake of success, get ready, because a fall is looming.

Loss of success may not be the principal cause in the spike of economy-related suicides in our world today. The spike could also be a result of bruised egos, loss of not just material possessions and hope, but loss of pride, resulting in an increase in shame. Once we allow our sense of self to become tied to our job, when the job goes away so does our identity. We will begin to view ourselves as less than nothing because in our minds, we have nothing left.

Stay balanced. Success is good. Ambition is good. It is the loss of perspective that is bad.

Status — the Boastful Pride of Life
Me, Myself and I

I am so wonderful, just take a look and see.
I am as close to perfect as anyone can be.

Just look at my house, even look at my car,
I am so much better than all of you are.

My degree is from one of the top tier schools,
I didn't go local like the rest of you fools.

I don't wear cheap shoes, unlike you,
I wear nothing but the best, Blahniks or Choo.

I have so much money, but I give none away,
Who knows when I will have a rainy day?

I don't apologize for having it all,
I will never have to beg, borrow, or crawl.

I am so wonderful, just take a look and see.
Too bad everyone can't be like me.

Do you know anyone like this? Are *you* like this? Of course, most people are not as bold to say these kinds of things aloud, but remember lust is an inside job. They may not say them, but their actions scream them. Of the Big Three, vainglory or the boastful pride of life is the most insidious and self-destructive, and one that God hates (see Proverbs 6:17). Those who love to boast about what they have, do so from a place of insecurity and fear, not security and strength. Even though they come across as the most confident people in the world, most of the time, it is just a bluff and a shield to keep others from probing deeper. This person will have a tight inner circle sometimes even just a circle of one — themselves. They will never allow anyone to get close enough to peer beneath the thin veneer of boldness, success, self-confidence, and perfection. Even those who think they know these kinds of people really don't know them at all, because they will only allow you to know what they want you to know.

Their security and strength is not in God, not even in themselves, but in what they possess and what they can portray that they possess. There are deeper underlying issues and dynamics at play with status seekers and status keepers.

The downfall of a status seeker/keeper can be brutal, sometimes fatal — fatal because some will go to any lengths to protect their carefully crafted image. In the extreme, they may even, like the young man mentioned earlier, step in front of a moving train or choose some other method of ending it all. They would rather die than to have anyone discover that their life is far from the picture perfect one they portray, especially if they are living a lie based upon past glory. All glory is fleeting and when it goes, the status seeker may want to go with it.

So, how do you avoid this? Stay humble and honest — with you. When you look into the mirror, I mean *really* look into the mirror, and don't like who or what you have become, as I mentioned earlier, make a date with yourself and have a long, introspective, reflective conversation over dinner, with you. This will seem strange and uncomfortable at first. When you have determined to do it, the first thing you will be tempted to do is talk yourself out of it. You have become accustomed to and practiced at operating efficiently and proficiently from the outside in. This forces you to work from the inside out. Your problem isn't on the outside, in fact, the outside is perfect. It is the inside that is putrid.

Secondly, as status seekers and keepers, we are tightly wound emotionally and sharing is difficult. We can share dinner, lunch or small talk, and may be consummate hosts or hostesses. We love people; we just won't allow people to love us back.

This brings me to my final point; if this describes you, find someone in whom you can confide even if it is a mental health professional. Our secrets can hold us emotionally hostage and can be our harshest critics. I am not talking about sharing every indiscretion since second grade. I am talking about sharing with someone trustworthy those things in your professional life that are affecting your personal life, and those things affecting your personal life that are causing you to operate hypocritically in your professional life.

Eventually, it will all come out in the wash and your house of duplicity and deception will come crashing down. This is especially important if you are a leader in any capacity. We are not designed to contain pain. It will eventually surface and when it does, it often isn't pretty. There are no cloaks of anonymity anymore and it is getting more difficult by the day to keep up pretenses and veneers. When the pretenses are discovered and the veneer is painfully stripped away, the fallout and unavoidable fall will be unforgivable for some and stunningly unexpected to all.

Is the Risk *Really* Worth the Reward?

So my friend, count the costs. This is the longest chapter of the book because these are the most deadliest and vulnerable areas of our humanity. Our downfall will likely be tied to one or a combination of these three. Some of us will lie, cheat, steal and kill for them. What Kryptonite is to Superman, these are to you and me. They are the areas where we are the weakest, and where we will be most tempted by the enemy.

If we succumb to their powerful lure, personal pain, public shame, or both are not very far behind. The bigger we are, the bigger they are. And they have precipitated the downfall of some of the most influential, charismatic, political and religious leaders, sports figures, and entertainers of our time. No one is immune; there is no discrimination, as they will do the same for ordinary people like you and me.

Whether your bait is sex (lust of the flesh), stuff (lust of the eyes), status (boastful pride of life), or any combination of the three in any degree, before biting, even nibbling, consider the risks. Never underestimate the risks and never underestimate the power of the lure.

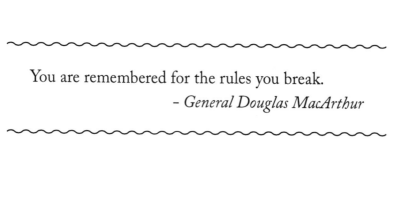

You are remembered for the rules you break.
- *General Douglas MacArthur*

I never intended to break any rule.

Now I feel like such a fool.

Everyone trusted me and I let them down.

No one at all now wants me around.

I needed the money but got carried away.

I would have paid it back someday.

I am so ashamed and my family is too.

It's over, I'm done, my career is through.

CHAPTER 6

❦

RULING OUT THE RULES:
THE PRICE IS ALWAYS HIGHER THAN THE COST.

"Ill-gotten gains do not profit, But righteousness delivers from death."

Proverbs 10:2

Have you ever worked or served with someone who thought the rules applied to everyone but them? I once worked with a gentleman who was and remains a high-level government employee. One of his favorite sayings and one he took pride in was, "I don't break the rules, but I sure bend the hell out of them."

Sadly, this appears to be the prevailing attitude throughout our culture, not just in government but also in business, academia, civic organizations, even in some places of worship. It appears as though the rules are always for the other guy.

If we lived in Utopia, everyone would follow all the rules all the time. That is just not how the real world works. We all are rule breakers and if anyone tries to convince you otherwise, just know they are breaking one of the cardinal rules — honesty. No one walks the straight and narrow all the time — no one. Most of us have rolled through a STOP sign or two, sneaked a peek over a classmate's shoulder at test time, or grazed in the produce section while shopping at the local grocery.

However, the rules and laws we break that can end our careers, permanently stain our reputations, and call into question our ethics, credibility, and integrity are much more odious than these and the list can stretch for pages.

Victory at the ballot box, longevity in leadership, professional and even volunteer positions do not give us a free pass. As we become more comfortable in our roles and positions, we will become more comfortable with breaking the rules and the rule of law.

No one runs for political office with the intent of ending up busted, broke, and embarrassed, sitting in a dank prison cell having taken a bribe that in the end was worth only pennies — certainly not worth a stellar reputation and career.

No one volunteers to serve as church treasurer, PTA, or booster club president to end up being indicted for raiding the cookie dough account to steal funds meant to purchase new choir robes or football equipment. What police officer goes through the rigors of police training academy with visions of someday being handcuffed and hauled off to jail for selling dope to an undercover officer? Yet these kinds of things and worse happen and are happening more frequently.

The rules we make or the laws we swear to uphold apply to us as they do everyone. No one is above the law and eventually rule breakers are caught. The law of averages catches up with the best of us. In the case of those in position to make the rules; it is disappointing, alarming, and shameful when the rule maker becomes the rule breaker.

When it comes to ruling out the rules, there is no special category. None of us is above it, from the grocery store clerk boosting cash from the cash register to the CEO embezzling millions from his or her corporation. Over time, it becomes easier and easier to skim money off the top, take another bribe or embezzle another million. However, there is always a hefty price to pay. That price most often comes in the form of an embarrassing investigation and perhaps an indictment and conviction.

The price could be the hurtful shun of friends and colleagues as they turn their backs on you; and you're left out in the cold - locked out of a life and lifestyle you had immensely enjoyed. However, the steepest price of all is the sacrifice and loss of a good name.

161

Several years ago, the movie *What's Love Got To Do With It,* portrayed the life of the legendary Tina Turner. While there were many riveting scenes in the movie, the one that was the most striking to me came near the end during her and Ike's divorce proceeding. The one thing Tina (brilliantly portrayed by Angela Basset) was concerned about and was adamant about was retaining her name.

For years, even though she had been by far the shining star of the duo, she had been horrifically humiliated, used, and abused by Ike. As she sat proudly and boldly in the divorce hearing, she told the judge she didn't want Ike's money or anything else, except her name. Nearing the end of the proceedings, the judge looked sternly at her and said, "you're gonna walk out of here with absolutely nothing." This was the part that made me jump up and shout. She had come through literal hell with Ike, and when the judge said that, Tina defiantly retorted, "Except my name." You go, girl!

When we rule out the rules and break the rule of law for whatever reason, the saddest part of all is that we don't take into account the fact that a good name is better than all the riches in the world (see Proverbs 22:1). We can always make more money, build another house, buy another car, or buy more new clothes; but the one thing we can never buy back is our name. When we stain our name — no matter how wealthy, talented or philanthropic we become — we will go to our grave with that invisible asterisk next to our name along with a footnote in the annals of history.

For example, if I mention Richard Nixon, what comes to mind? Likewise, if I mention Kenneth Lay, what comes to mind? The list could go on. While Richard Nixon wasn't the only figure in the Watergate scandal, he was the face of it and it cost him the presidency. Likewise, Kenneth Lay wasn't the only culprit in the meltdown of Enron; however, he will forever be blamed for it.

No matter whatever else we accomplish or do that is good, right, and wholesome, like General MacArthur so famously said, we will be remembered for the rules we break. While we may someday be able to restore our image, we may never be able to restore our standing; and if we do, the asterisk will still be there because someone, in some setting, will always recall it. It is like spilling red wine on white carpet. You can clean the carpet, but a hint of the stain will remain and if the stain is bad enough, the carpet will have to be replaced. When we are stained badly enough, we too will have to be replaced.

While the rules we break and the laws we disregard can be significant, some of the more prevalent ones that those in leadership or other trusted positions violate are listed below. This list is not at all intended to be exhaustive or mutually exclusive, only a fair representation of the kinds of rules and rules of law that when cavalierly disregarded and skirted, begin a downward spiral into the abyss of guilt, shame and despair for not only us, but for our families:

- Record tampering

- Mail fraud

- Racketeering

- Tax evasion

- Embezzlement

- Abuse of authority

- Public corruption

- Money laundering

- Ethics violations

- Forgery

- Wire fraud

- Conflicts of interest

- Kickbacks

- Obstruction of justice

- Perjury

- Padded resumes

- Bribery

- Extortion

- Conspiracy

- Credit card abuse

- Theft

SINGING FROM THE SAME P.A.G.E.

While some thrive on pushing the envelope and walking dangerously close to the edge, when rule breakers rule out the rules it isn't for the thrill of clandestine meetings, twisted plots, or the exhilarating thought of adventure. For these, they are in it to score one of four things: 1) money; 2) goods; 3) services or, 4) preferential treatment.

For those who have a bent toward bending and breaking the rules, they will risk being tried in a court of law and the court of public opinion for these four in a heartbeat even though at the time, that may be the furthest thing from their mind. In fact, we will explore this later. But there are some experienced rule breakers who have so convinced themselves that there is absolutely nothing wrong with what they are doing or have done that when confronted, they are offended.

While we typically think of the fat cat politician or the corporate tycoon type who break the rules for the sake of having more, there are those who are now risking it all, not out of greed, but necessity. For these, it isn't about scoring an extra million or an all expense paid trip. It is about keeping food on the table and the lights turned on.

Desperation can make decent people do desperate things. I am not excusing their behavior and actions, nor attempting to explain it away; however, it is just a reality of the times in which we live. People are hurting and are willing to take chances they never dreamed they would be forced to take, praying, and hoping that things turn around before the money they take to buy groceries or pay the mortgage is discovered missing. When they are caught (it is always just a matter of time) the shame and humiliation can be almost unbearable. These, however, are the exceptions and not the rule.

For the most part, people who routinely rule out the rules are usually singing from the same P.A.G.E. While they may be in totally different areas — government, business, entertainment, or sports, they usually share the same attributes and tendencies that lead to them throwing away well-established careers and reputations.

It would be foolish and irresponsible on my part to pigeon-hole and throw everyone into the same category. However, it has been my experience that people who are unafraid to jeopardize their name, career, credibility, ethics and standing in the community, in order to illegally obtain money, goods, services, and preferential treatment, exhibit the same four qualities. I call it singing from the same P.A.G.E.

PRIDE — ARROGANCE — GREED — EGO

What is so insidious when it comes to these four is that most people whose lives have been uprooted and wrecked by them will often ask, "Why didn't I see this coming?" or, "Why didn't somebody tell me I had gotten to be such a ..." I won't write the word because this is a family friendly book, but you get the idea.

The answer is this, and it is as simple as I can make it. Unless we have someone to point out to us that we have become puffed up with pride, that we have become arrogant, greedy or egotistical, we will never see it for ourselves. By then, however, it is far too late because once we have become proud, arrogant, greedy, or egotistical, we likely are not going to surround ourselves with people who will tell us. P.A.G.E. people can't stand to hear that kind of naked truth. Even if they did, by the time they have become corrupted by pride and arrogance, they are not willing to listen. It is a Catch-22.

They are not willing to listen because proud people don't want to be told they are proud. Arrogant people don't want to be told they are arrogant. Greedy people become offended if you tell them they are greedy; and, egotistical people will tune out the message altogether because it doesn't feed their ego.

Anything or anybody that doesn't feed the ego of the egotist won't be part of their inner circle for very long. Unlike pride, arrogance and greed, that can stand alone; ego needs to feed off something and most of the time it feeds off pride. The more proud we are, the bigger our ego will become.

Not only does God hate arrogance (see Proverbs 6:17), but He opposes proud people (see 1 Peter 5:5). I would rather be opposed by a herd of raging bulls that hadn't eaten in a week, than be opposed by God. Pride is a prelude to a fall (see Proverbs 16:18). There is no way around it. When it comes to greed, Jesus warns against it in Luke 12:15: "Then He said to them, "Beware, and be on your guard against every form against of greed; for not *even* when one has an abundance does his life consist of his possessions."

So how can you tell when you are walking dangerously close to the precipice and are about to take a tumble? What does pride, arrogance, greed, and ego look like? How can you tell when you have gotten to the point where you are gullible or arrogant enough to believe you can break the rules and succeed where others have failed? Where do you draw the line? How do you know when you are about to take a kamikaze hit to your reputation, credibility and name because you have become so engulfed by these almost stealth sins?

Let's take a closer look at pride, arrogance, greed, and ego and explore how they trick us into thinking we are above the rules, can bend the rules; and, can get away with breaking the rules. The most deadly of these is pride as it is the mother of all others.

Pride — A False Sense of Security

One of the drawbacks of excellence is that we have the tendency to believe we *are* excellent. When in fact, it is not us that are excellent. but the ability we have that allows us to be excellent at what we do. Only God can claim excellence. Our ability comes from Him, not us. When we allow the greatness of what we do to make us believe we are great, we have become prideful.

One of the reasons God hates pride (see Proverbs 6:16-17) and will leave us twisting in the wind when we become prideful is because we will begin to believe that because of our ability, resources, influence, power, wealth and popularity, we can handle anything that comes our way. That sends a message to God that we can run our life without Him. We in essence declare our independence from Him. When we declare our independence from Him, we also are declaring independence from His protection.

We will begin to rely more on our money than our Maker. When this happens, we develop a false sense of security. When we develop a false sense of security, we will begin to believe we are our own god and that we make things happen; further, that we have the last say over any situation and that the buck truly stops with us. When we begin to believe we are bulletproof, we will take foolish chances and do foolish things, because, like fools, we will develop a false sense of security whereby we will believe that not even God can touch us.

We soon will begin making strategic mistakes. Prosperity and power can lead to pride and corruption. Among other things, we will become involved in dirty deals, demand that others bow to us, pay to play with us, and that they pay their dues to us. After all, we are top dog, and who is to say differently? The fall from the top — for top dogs who have come to believe they are top dogs of their own making — is a long and embarrassing one. When we become so secure in ourselves that we get beside ourselves, we are setting up ourselves to stumble and stumble badly.

BELIEVING OUR OWN PRESS

Everyone loves to have good things said about them. However, when we take flattery for more than what it is — likely a way to get our attention or curry favor — we will begin to see ourselves through the warped lenses of flattery rather than through the clear lenses of reality. Flattery is fine. However, we should allow it to go in one ear and out the other. Otherwise, we will retain it all and as a result, begin to become overconfident in our abilities, positions, accomplishments, and achievements. The end result is pride.

Proud people love to be praised, and will follow praise right over a cliff. Popularity is never permanent. The more popular we become, the more vulnerable we become, because popularity has an intoxicating way of breeding a sense of invincibility and pride. When we become so popular and prideful that we believe we are invincible, a fall is looming.

Don't be fooled by accolades. You can go to bed a genius and wake up a goat. People are selfish and unless you seek wisdom from God, it is difficult to discern if people are sincere or not sincere. The safest thing to do is to pay little attention to criticism and even less to compliments. Without you knowing it, people will, for their own comfort, convenience, and motives pump you up into believing you are the greatest thing since sliced bread. When that happens and when we begin believing this distorted view of ourselves, we will begin overestimating our own sense of importance. An overestimation of importance always leads to an over exaggeration of ability.

Recognizing we don't have the juice that people think we have will cause us to break any rule we feel needed to save face. This includes taking credit for someone else's work, accomplishments, ideas or padding our resume with experiences we have never had. Because of pride, we will think nothing of flaunting all of these as our own. However, there is always a reckoning day. A padded resume can only go undetected for so long before someone begins asking questions or senses incongruence.

Pride so craves recognition that it will drive us to go to any length to obtain it, no matter how fraudulently. The end result is always the same as the truth is invariably uncovered — loss of integrity and loss of respect, with zero credibility.

PRIDE AND PREJUDICE

Pride and prejudice are joined at the hip. Prejudice is rooted in personal pride in a quest for personal power. Whether we realize it or not, recognize it or not, accept it or not, or believe it or not; the same God that created us, created our worst enemy, our most hated rival and our most hated race or culture of people. For some of us, that is hard to wrap our head around. We would rather believe that "they" were spawned from alien eggs, not created by the God we claim to love, worship, and serve. If that is your view, not only do you have a warped sense of who God is, but a serious distortion of who you are.

We are reminded in Romans 12:3 not to think more highly of ourselves than we ought to think. Yet, when we engage in any type of "ism," whether it is elitism, racism, or self-righteousness, we are doing just that.

Anytime we hold others in contempt, think ourselves better, cruelly mistreat, despise or look down our noses on others that are racially different from us, we have become prejudiced and prideful. Not only that, we have insulted God *and* Jesus because Colossians 1:16 tells us that by Him all things were created, not only by Him but for Him — all things, all people.

When it comes to the "isms," racism is by far the most prevalent in America. The ugly history of race in this country is still being written. Ruling out the rules of human decency and ruling out the rule of law has been the norm when it comes to race. Racial superiority, rooted in pride, has caused the loss of life for some, imprisonment for others, and ostracism for still others.

Since by definition racism is racial pride which gives rise to feelings of superiority over others based strictly upon race, then it stands to reason that no one race has the corner market on racism. This has absolutely nothing to do with racial politics, or conservative versus liberal.

If you believe you are superior to another because of your race, that constitutes racism — it doesn't matter what race you are. I will use myself as an example. If I believe that my being black makes me better than my neighbor who is Hispanic, that is racism. If you are white and based upon being white, you believe you are superior to me because I am black, that is racism. Prejudice, no matter from whom it emanates, is rooted in pride — black pride, white pride, Hispanic pride it is all the same. While the quest for personal power can lead to an all-consuming racial hatred, it can also lead to an all-consuming meltdown.

ON THE SAME SINKING BOAT

There is an Italian proverb I have come to love, quote often and one that I have incorporated into my daily living because it keeps things in perspective for me:

"At the end of the game,
the pawn and the king go back in the same box."

It doesn't matter how elite we believe ourselves to be. Death is the great equalizer. In the end, it won't matter if we are laid out in a diamond-studded platinum box with down interior, or if we are laid out in a cardboard box lined with yellowing newspaper. The lid is going to be shut and our bodies are going to be worm food or if cremated, reduced to ashes, scattered to the wind or piled in an urn like ashes from last winter's fire. Even more, the kicker is this, the same people we look down on in this life may be the same people we will have to look up to in the life to come because the Bible says that the last shall be first, and the first shall be last (see Matthew 20:16).

Not only is it a sin to think more highly of ourselves than we ought to think; but it is absolutely foolhardy to look down our nose on others because we may have more expensive toys, live in a bigger house, and, drive a Ferrari instead of a Ford.

It is equally foolish to consider ourselves above others simply because of the number of letters behind our name. Elitism is a dangerous road to tread. When we become puffed up with pride based upon our belief that we are entitled to or deserve special treatment by virtue of our perceived superiority, we will begin to feel a sense of entitlement to be enjoyed only by us — the elite, while everyone else be damned.

We clamor and claw to be part of the society scene, basing our worth on the opinions of people just like us. However, social winds change; and they *will* change because the pendulum always swings back. When for whatever reason, we find ourselves suddenly on the outs — when we are as out as we once were in — then we're ready to jump out of the nearest window, hang ourselves from the highest rafter, or shoot ourselves in the head.

It doesn't matter how wealthy, blue-blooded, talented or educated we are, in the end, none of us can afford the price of elitism, not in this world or the world to come.

What Would Jesus Do?

Jesus had one word for self-righteous people — hypocrites. Self-righteousness is particularly offensive to the faith it claims to represent. If anyone piously and judgmentally looks down his or her nose on others in the smug name of religion, that's not faith-based anything, that is pride-based prejudice.

Only God knows a person's heart. Therefore, it is the height of arrogance for anyone to judge anyone else based upon his or her narrow-minded view of religion giving no thought at all to spirituality. It is easy to be religious but not spiritual; meaning, you base your faith and actions on ritualistic laws and rigid, religious rules, developed by your interpretation of what God said in His word, without bothering to become knowledgeable enough *about* His word to fully understand what He meant when He said it. Therefore, when we put our spin on what we think He meant, and base our opinions and actions on that, we take on the role of a mini god, judging people based upon our narrow interpretation of what we think, rather than what God meant.

It was the religious people of His day that were hell-bent on crucifying Jesus, not the regular people. It is the religious people today that are still in the crucifying business. God loves us all, but hates our sin. He begins with love and ends with love. The self-righteous begins with hate and ends with hate. Oh, we wouldn't dare call it that, but that is what it is. We misjudge people, taunt people, mislead and misguide people, label people, taint people's names, lie on people, use people, disregard people, malign people all in the name of religion.

For those of us who self-righteously judge and nonchalantly kick people to the curb, there will come a day when the righteous Judge will judge. What would Jesus do? I don't know. But I do know what He said he would say to the hypocrites on judgment day, "I never knew you, depart from me," (Matt. 7:23). Will He say the same of you?

Pride Means Never Having to Say You're Sorry

We can't leave this section without focusing on a key aspect of pride that I don't want you to miss. This is often overlooked but is key if you are not going to allow pride to wreck your career or credibility; or, if you are struggling to understand a proud person in your life.

Proud people rarely apologize or admit wrong. Admission of guilt or fault is not in their DNA and is a major reason why they choose to ignore, bend, or break the rules. They could be caught red-handed and still will not admit wrong. Why? Because the admission of wrong requires humility and humility is seen by the proud as a weakness and not a strength. Since God gives grace to the humble but opposes the proud (see 1 Peter 5:5), what the proud sees as a weakness is really a strength; but in the long run for them what they view as a strength (refusal to be humble) will turn out to be a liability.

The higher up on the food chain, the more difficult it becomes to say, "I'm sorry." "I was wrong." "Can you please forgive me?" Unless there is a heart change, that is just not going to happen. However, it is always to *their* detriment and not to the one whom they wronged. To be fair it is not always that the proud doesn't *want* to apologize; they may not see a *need* to apologize because they honestly believe they have done nothing wrong. If that is their reality, and it is, then they don't have a need to apologize.

That is why people, who don't understand pride and how it can consume a person, react so negatively toward politicians who have been caught red-handed yet still offer a defense of innocence. Again, I am not excusing the behavior, just trying to explain it. In their way of thinking, they *are* innocent because they honestly believe that whatever it was they did, it was within their purview to do.

Since proud people find it difficult to admit wrong, it leads to disagreements, dissension, conflict, and contention, both in their personal and professional lives. It causes them to lash out at others who likely are purely innocent whose only crime was getting in their way. When threatened, they jump quickly into self-preservation mode, where ruling out all rules is the order of the day. They will throw their most trusted advisor under the bus if it will save them. The proud often resort to putting others down, while falsely accusing still others in an attempt to redirect the spotlight from them. Nothing else matters except holding on to the power and prestige of their position, by any means necessary. However, people cheer when they invariably are knocked from their throne. The prouder they have been, the louder the cheers, because people love to see proud people get their due.

Learn to be humble because humility may someday be your saving grace.

Arrogance

The most salient difference between pride and arrogance is that unlike pride, arrogance is a self-centered high-mindedness, based not upon possessions, position, prestige, race, or things outside of itself. Arrogance is based upon internal qualities that we believe make us special, unique and superior. It could be our talent, looks, body, special skill, quality, ability, or intellect. An arrogant person is self-contained, meaning they don't require anything outside of themselves to make them feel good about themselves, because everything about them is already far superior than anything that could possibly be added to make them better. Accolades or no accolades, flattery or no flattery, doesn't make them a dime's bit of difference. They know they have it going on, and whether they are complimented or not is irrelevant. Arrogance and cockiness are two sides of the same coin.

Arrogant people rule out the rules by failing to heed warnings or advice. No one can tell them anything because they already know it all. Hardheaded used to be the term, but whatever it is called, you can advise a truly arrogant person until the cows come home and they will still walk right into a buzz saw.

Greed

The story is told of a little dog walking across a narrow bridge with a nice-sized bone. As he approached the middle of the bridge, he peeped over the edge into the babbling brook below. He saw another dog staring back at him with what looked to be a bigger bone. Up until seeing the other dog's bone, he was perfectly content with the bone he had. Now seeing the bigger bone, he had to have it. He dove into the brook, opened his mouth to snatch the bigger bone from the other dog and when he did, he lost his bone and was forced to watch helplessly as his bone floated away. He ended up with neither bone because what he thought was another dog with a bigger bone was merely his reflection.[1]

Greed will cause us to lose what we have in an attempt to gain more. Those who are prone to greed will rule out the rules and will think nothing of ruling out the rule of law. Greed fosters a sense of entitlement, whereby we feel it is our right to take a bribe, steal, embezzle, cheat on our taxes and do whatever we have to do in order to get whatever we feel we have to have.

Most of the people caught in white-collar sting operations are not homeless or on welfare. They are mostly professional people, making decent incomes including perks. We become blinded by an excessive desire for more money, more prestige, more possessions, and a better position, and will not be denied. Our insatiable desire for these will cause us to overlook the obvious warning signs and plunge head first into the pool of prosperity never bothering to test the temperature of the water.

Greed will drive us to become preoccupied with possessions and deceive us into thinking the grass is always greener on the other side. We won't stop to realize, however, if the grass is greener, the water bill is going to be higher too.

It is a dangerous thing to want what someone else has. In the first place, we never know the sacrifices that person had to make to have what they have and secondly, we can never be sure what kind of activities they are participating in to keep it.

The meltdown of the housing market and the Wall Street implosion were due primarily to greed. People lost life savings by pouring money down a black hole in order to purchase a home they could never, in two lifetimes, afford. Greed thrives where there is gullibility. There will always be gullible people because there will always be greedy people. The disadvantage of greed is that we never know when we have had enough, because with greed, enough is never enough and the more we get, the more we want.

The key to fighting greed is learning to become content with what you have.

EGO

We all have an ego, but what keeps most of our egos in check is humility and reality. Since ego feeds off pride, you can be poor as a church mouse and have a big ego. However, that is the exception and not the rule.

Generally speaking, those with overly inflated egos have an overly exaggerated and skewed view of their self-importance. Egos are not gender specific. There are women I know with egos so big that their body and their ego can barely squeeze through the door together.

An ego will force us to rule out the rules and the rule of law, if it means helping to maintain our status and image. Status and image are the two drivers behind overly inflated egos. The fear of losing status in the eyes of others can cause egotistical people to take some unusually dangerous risks in order to protect and maintain their status. They will break whatever rule they have to break, even the law if it helps them keep up with what amounts to a morbid game of charades.

Since the egoist is more concerned about what others think, he or she may lie, cheat, beg, borrow, and steal in order to maintain a lifestyle that supports their ego; long after they can afford no longer to keep up the pretenses. Because of pride, conceit, and self-centeredness, appearance takes precedent over substance. It is all about keeping up appearances for appearance sake.

Watch your ego, because it will take you places you never wanted to go, even worse, places from which you may not be able to return.

We all break the rules every now and then and like my former colleague, at times even seriously bend them. However, it is embarrassing when the rule maker becomes the rule breaker. Even more, breaking the rule of law can cost us that which we have worked so hard to earn — a great career, a promising future, a sterling reputation and even more a good name.

Spare yourself and your family this humiliation. Follow the rules — don't bend them, don't break them and don't cover for those who do.

Life's tragedy is that we get old too soon and wise too late.

– *Benjamin Franklin*

I'll get angry in a minute, at the drop of a hat.

Don't mess with me or I'll grab my bat.

I've always had things just my way.

I could care less about what people might say.

No one can tell me what to do,

Not my family, not my friends, not even you.

I do what I want because my life is my own

You can't tell me a thing I'm grown.

CHAPTER 7

~∂

EMOTIONAL IMMATURITY: GROWN BUT NOT GROWN UP

"How blessed is the man who finds wisdom And the man who gains understanding."

Proverbs 3:13

There is a Cherokee tale about a young boy who went to his grandfather because he was angry to the point of hatred because a friend had done him an injustice. The grandfather calmly sat the young man down and said, "Son, let me tell you a story."

"Over the years, I too at times have felt great anger and hatred for those that have taken so much from me with no sorrow for what they do. But hate wears you down and does not hurt your enemy. It is like taking poison and wishing your enemy would die. I have struggled with these feelings many times," he continued.

"It is as if there are two wolves inside me. One is good and does no harm. He lives in harmony with all around him, and does not take offense when no offense was intended. He will only fight when it is right to do so, and in the right way.

But the other wolf, ah! He is full of anger. The littlest thing will set him into a fit of rage. He fights everyone, all the time, and for no good reason. He cannot think because his anger and hate are so great. It is useless anger, for his anger changes nothing.

Sometimes, it is hard to live with these two wolves inside me, for both of them try to dominate my spirit."

The boy looked intently into his Grandfather's eyes and asked, "Which one wins, Grandfather?"

The Grandfather smiled, looked at the boy, and quietly said, "The one I feed."

We all have the same two wolves, even though I am sure if you're like me, you likely know a few people who host a pack of them. You're never quite sure which wolf is going to show up, so you have learned to wait to see if they come baring teeth or wagging tail. You have learned to allow them to make the first move or say the first hello lest you risk having your head bitten off and handed back to you. Even tougher is when we live with wolf daddy or wolf mama. Life is not much fun.

What if, however, the roles were reversed? What if people shied away from us or felt the need to walk on eggshells around us because of our emotional unpredictability? Much of the volatility in relationships whether marital, professional, or personal is brought about because of emotional immaturity.

Emotional immaturity has little to do with age, but everything to do with self-control, self-confidence, and balance.

Nothing will precipitate a downfall faster than when people find it difficult to work with you, work for you, serve with you, or be married to you because they are never quite sure which one of you is going to show up.

Trust is key in any relationship. In order for people to trust you, they have to be comfortable with you and in order for them to be comfortable with you, they have to have confidence in you. If they don't have confidence in you, they are not going to keep you around very long. If an employee, you eventually will end up getting the boot; if a politician, you will end up being booted from office; and if married, you will end up being booted out of the house.

The one thing that increases the comfort level of others is your predictability. I am not saying you should walk around as a robot or droid, but what I am saying is that if you are not at a place of maturity and you still wear your emotions on your sleeve, and fly off the handle at the drop of a hat, you are not going to be very successful.

People are not going to waste time coddling you or trying to understand you because people are busy and there are too many other people out there who would take the opportunity you have been given and run with it. Intelligence, a college degree, looks, pedigree, or performance will be trumped every time by temperament. Temperament undermines talent. One of the greatest assets you and I will ever have is the ability to get along well with people. It doesn't matter if you're the President or the postman — people are key to our success or failure, because wherever we go, they are going to be there too.

Are people going to get on your nerves? Yes they are, to the point that you may want to strangle them. We all have had those days. What I have learned and what I want you to know is that while people may push your buttons, no one but you can push you over the edge. They may push, but you don't have to budge.

When we are not emotionally mature enough to handle the inevitable pressure of people, we are going to fail every time. It isn't situations or circumstances that cause us the most grief, it is people. People create situations and circumstances, not the other way around. How we respond and react will determine the heights to which we climb or the depths to which we sink. By far, the most hurtful downfalls are those we bring upon ourselves by our inability to control ourselves. There is no wound so deep as the one we inflict upon ourselves. If we learn to master these three areas — self-control, self-confidence; and balance, there is no limit to how far we can go. One thing is guaranteed, if we don't mature to the point of mastering them, we will always be mastered by those who have.

Self-control — Learning to Control Our Tongues

There is no way to master self-control until we first learn to master what we say. The Bible calls the tongue "a restless evil and full of deadly poison" (James 3:8). Behind every word we utter is a spiritual element spoken for a spiritual purpose of which sometimes we are not even aware — principally, to cut, destroy, build up or encourage — even if we are cutting, destroying, building up or encouraging ourselves.

When I began studying about the tongue as it relates to emotional maturity, and began to study more deeply in order to gain a better understanding of the implications of what we say, why we say what we say, and, what prompts us to say what we say; I found it nothing short of fascinating.

When we speak to an issue, we are either being used as instruments of God or instruments of Satan. What prompted me to look more closely at this premise was an exchange between Peter and Jesus. As Jesus was explaining to the disciples why he had to go to Jerusalem to be crucified, Peter took Jesus aside and told him in essence that could never be, presumably out of concern. Jesus, the Bible says, sharply rebuked

Peter. This is the part that intrigued me. After Peter told Jesus in essence He didn't have to go to the cross, Jesus looked right at Peter and said, "Get behind me, Satan! You are a stumbling block to me..." (Matt. 16:23). The last thing Satan wanted was the crucifixion and resurrection of Jesus the Christ. Therefore, knowing he couldn't come to Jesus straight up, he used one that was close to Him for this dastardly purpose. We will talk more about this later, but he continues even today to use those closest to us, oftentimes unbeknownst to us, to thwart the plan and purpose of God for our life. That is why the Bible teaches us to try the spirits so we can discern which is which.

In reading the exchange between Peter and Jesus, I said to myself, "wait a minute, wasn't it Peter who was talking?" While the words were coming out of Peter's mouth, it was Satan who was speaking them *through* Peter. This may sound radical to some, but when we are speaking to other people, or about other people, or, to issues involving other people; we are either being used by God to build up and encourage or misused by Satan to cut and destroy. What is so frightening is most of the time we are completely unaware, as was Peter.

What I am about to say may seem totally off the wall to some, but in order for us to move into emotional maturity when it comes to our tongue, it is imperative that we understand the spiritual aspects of our tongue and the spiritual ramifications.

We can cause our own downfall by the words that come out of our mouth. Everything we see and hear becomes a permanent part of our memory bank. While we may never actively think on these things, particularly the most hurtful ones (i.e., "you'll never be anything," "you're no good just like your daddy," "you're dumb," "you're stupid," "you're fat..."), they nonetheless become part of us and can serve as the genesis for our downfall or failure decades down the road. That is why we should be careful about what we speak and how we speak into the lives of our children. Because of our own immaturity or ignorance (and I say that in love) in this area, we could not only be speaking death into their lives but could be setting them up as adults to fail.

Satan is the prince of the power of the air (see Ephesians 2:2). He hears every word that is spoken to us and by us. He hears every mindless utterance and it sets the stage for him at some point in the future, when we least expect it and in venues we least expect, to bring life to those utterances, but only if they are destructive in some way to us. Be wary of what you say, because our words are seeds. We speak them into the atmosphere, the prince of the power of the air picks them up, and like the spiritual seeds they are, he plants them in the fertile soil of our minds. As seeds do, they stay there, germinate, and grow into thoughts. We learn in Proverbs 18:21 that death and life are in the power of the tongue and that we will bear the consequences of the words we speak for good or for bad. When thoughts have been planted into your mind such as:

"You can't do anything right."
"They need to pay us more money. I just hate it here, don't you?"
"You'll never be able to go to college, who are you kidding?"
"I put food on the table working this job.
If it was good enough for me, it's good enough for you..."
and on and on.

Such thoughts will take root in your mind and germinate. This is a crucial point. The choice is to discard or dismiss them right away or to allow them to take hold. If we allow them to roll over and over in our minds, we will eventually speak them out of our mouth. That is just the way we are wired. That is why the Apostle Paul in Philippians 4:8 tells us this: "Finally, brethren, whatever is true, whatever is honorable, whatever is right, whatever is pure, whatever is lovely, whatever is of good repute...**dwell** on these things."

Whatever we dwell on in our mind is going to eventually come out of our mouth or in our actions. We are either speaking good, right or honorable things, which will bring good, right or honorable things to us; or, we are speaking depressing, negative, and trashy things, which will bring depressing, negative, and trashy things to us. When we repeat the lies of the enemy, and the negative thoughts that have been planted into our mind, that's when Satan says, "gotcha!" He knows, but without us realizing it, at that moment, we have just given life to those thoughts.

Even more, when we blurt out things that we in a million years wouldn't want anybody to even think we would think, let alone say, it's not by accident. That thought had always been there. As I said in the beginning of this discussion, once the seed has been planted, the stage is set. It is when we least expect it and in venues we least expect that those thoughts will come out of our mouth — and get this, remember it will always be when they can do the most damage and be the most destructive to us. We can apologize until the cows come home, but the damage has been done and can't be undone. You can hold some thoughts for years and never really think about them, but get famous or become high profile or a manager, CEO, or someone in an otherwise responsible position. What's more, it doesn't even have to be high profile. You can be just an employee and say something derogatory or backhanded to the boss, and guess what? You're out of a job.

Do you recall Howard Cosell or Jimmy "the Greek" Snyder? Both were legends in the field of sports broadcasting. Their downfall was a result of what came out of each of their mouth. What people call a slip of the tongue isn't a slip of the tongue at all. The words we hold in our minds will eventually be spoken out of our mouth; and sometimes, at the worst possible moment.

If you say you can't do anything right, you won't. If you say you are a sorry excuse for a man, you will begin carrying yourself that way, living that way, and you invariably will become just that. If you listen to your negative co-workers long enough as they consistently complain about their job, it won't be long before you'll begin finding fault with yours, even though before, you had no complaints whatsoever. If you say you'll never go to college, you won't. We give life to thoughts by speaking them into existence.

THE TONGUE THAT WOUNDS

The story is told of a little boy who had a bad temper. One day his dad gave him a bag of nails and told him that every time he lost his temper, he must hammer a nail into the back of their old fence.

The first day the boy had driven 37 nails into the fence. Over the next few weeks, as he learned to control his anger, the number of nails he hammered daily gradually dwindled. He discovered it was easier to hold his temper than to drive those nails into the fence.

Finally, the day came when the boy didn't lose his temper anymore. He proudly told his dad about it and his dad suggested that he now go out to the fence and pull out one nail for each day that he was able to hold his temper.

The days passed, and he was finally able to tell his dad that all the nails were gone. His dad took his son by the hand and led him to the fence.

He looked at the fence, and then looked at his son and he said, "You have done well son, but look at the holes in the fence. The fence will never be the same. When you say things in anger to wound, they leave a scar just like this one. You can put a knife in a man and draw it out. It won't matter how many times you say 'I'm sorry', the wound will still be there. A verbal wound son is just as bad as a physical one."[1]

When it comes to self-control, the ability to control our tongue as it relates to others is a litmus test of emotional maturity; and, one we all have failed many times on the path to maturity. More people have been wounded, reputations trashed, and careers damaged by uncontrolled tongues that foster divisiveness and cause damage and destruction that spread like wildfire. No one can stop the destruction once it starts. Before we speak, we should consider the following:

Is it true?

Is it kind?

Is it necessary?

Most of us could give a hill of beans about these three. However, this is the crux of the whole problem. Too many of us feel that gossip is great as long as it isn't about us. Slander is sweet as long as we can get away with it, and we die to tell a lie no matter how outlandish we know it to be. Some of us talk for the sake of hearing ourselves talk, never mind what is coming out of our mouth as long as we can join the jawing.

What is the motivation behind slander, gossip, manipulation, putting down others and twisting the truth? While they can be as varied as the people who engage in this kind of behavior, the common threads are these:

- Anger

- Envy

- Selfish ambition

- Resentment

- Bitter jealousy

- Destructive competitiveness

- Greed

- Hate

- Revenge

If we are honest with ourselves and if slander, gossip, twisting the truth, and cutting down someone in order to harm or damage their credibility, reputation, career, and name are par for the course for us, we will likely find our own motive reflected on this list. None of these are attributes of God, but of Satan. As such, when we slander, gossip and lie in order to harm, we are being misused by him, not used of God. I don't know about you, but I would rather be an instrument of God than an instrument of the enemy any day of the week. He is no friend to any of us and just as he uses us to cut and destroy others, there will come a time when he will use others to do the same to us, or likely, far worse.

Only God and we will ever know the truth. Others can only see our actions. And we can temper our hatred, jealousy, revenge, and anger with honey all we want, but God sees our heart. You can always tell the condition of a person's heart by what comes out of their mouth, no matter how holy they hold themselves out to be. The tongue lies, but the heart never does. What people say about others says more about them than the person they're speaking against.

Emotional maturity begins with the ability to control our tongue. If we cannot control our tongue, we will not be able to control our actions. If we can't control our actions because we are unable to control our tongue, it will be impossible to reach emotional maturity because self-control begins with our mouth.

SELF-CONTROL

Our mouth can bring about incredible blessings, dastardly curses, wonderful opportunities, or embarrassing downfalls. Control is key, but difficult. Like any obstacle we strive to overcome, learning to control our tongue so that we can move into a place of maturity will only come through practice, diligence, and perseverance.

While slandering, gossiping and maligning someone's character is anything but a game, make a game of it. Start keeping score of how many times you initiate or participate in these kinds of things and as each day goes by, try to participate one less time than you did yesterday or last week. It takes at least two to gossip but "for lack of wood the fire goes out, and where there is no whisperer, contention quiets down" (Prov. 26:20).

Not only will you begin to notice a difference in how you feel on the inside, but you also will begin to feel more confident and free. Gossip and slander are strongholds, and when they grip our heart and permeate our waking thoughts, they begin a slow but deliberate decaying process on the inside. Whether we realize it or not, every time we participate in tearing down another human being, we, in the process tear a little of ourselves down as well. We are all interconnected by way of our humanity. Even more, there is always a price to pay. Inexplicable things may begin happening. What we see as a run of bad luck or bad karma is not the case. We reap what we sow. As Dr. Charles Stanley, Senior Pastor of First Baptist Church Atlanta famously says, "we reap what we sow, later than we sow and more than we sow."

You can't slander and slam someone without reaping the same. An African proverb puts it this way, "ashes fly back into the face of him who throws them." God is not going to elevate a slanderer — Satan may, but God will not. If Satan elevates you, you will not only owe him your life, but your soul for all eternity. He is never late in collecting his debt nor does he accept late payments. The moment you sell out to him, he owns you. It could be that you have been cutting off your own blessings and promotion by cutting the legs out from underneath someone else — even anonymously.

There is no such thing as anonymous with God. He sees all, knows all, and will reward all according to our works. Don't think for a moment that just because you can hide behind the cloak of anonymity in the posting of anonymous, cutting, and slanderous comments on the Internet that you can hide behind the same when it comes to hiding from God. There is nothing or no one that escapes Him no matter how anonymous we make ourselves to be. We can fool some of the people all of the time, and all of the people some of the time, but we can't fool all of the people all of the time — and we can't fool God at any time.

The issue of the tongue has more spiritual implications than a lot of us know and a whole lot more than I can include here. Our words are powerful, and like a raging fire, are nearly impossible to control; and, all the more difficult to reverse the horrific damage they can cause.

SELF-CONFIDENCE

The way we view other people is a good indication of how we view ourselves. If we have healthy self-confidence, we won't feel the need to tear other people down in order to build ourselves up. Self-confidence comes from knowing who we are, appreciating who we are, and loving who we are. Self-confident people exude confidence and it is evident when they walk into a room. Being comfortable in our own skin means we won't be intimidated by others who are comfortable in theirs.

Self-confident people are usually emotionally mature people. If you are going to be self-confident, you're going to have to learn to put envy, fear, and doubt in their place. Only people with low self-esteem and low self-confidence allow themselves to be preoccupied with envying others while being fearful and doubtful of their own skills and abilities.

ENVY

Envy is foolish because it is based upon the misguided belief that someone else's success came at the expense of our own and we feel we are more deserving of the success than the object of our envy. Either way, it is a sign of low self-confidence and lack of emotional maturity.

If you really stopped to think about it, it's not the person you are envying who is the problem, it is you. Most of the time, in fact 99 times out of 100, if you were to be honest, the object of your envy has really done nothing to you at all — in fact, you likely have never held even a five-minute conversation with the person to get to know them. You only know what you think you see and you're envious of what you think you see and what you have heard — never bothering to check to make sure what you have heard is true. That's immaturity at its worst. Only children and fools take what people say at face value without checking the facts for themselves.

We envy when we measure what we see or think we see by whom we perceive ourselves to be, and in our minds, come up short. It is always easier to tear someone else down than to make the effort to build ourselves up. It is the cowardly, immature way of building our self-esteem on the cheap and at someone else's expense.

Even if the object of your envy were to drop dead in front of you, it wouldn't be long before there is someone to take his or her place. They were never the real problem.

It isn't that the other person thinks they are so much; it's that you think yourself to be so little. The way you see yourself will be the way you carry yourself and will be the way other people respond to and interact with you. If you see yourself as small and insignificant, you will walk, talk, and act small and insignificant; always esteeming others higher than you esteem yourself while hating every minute of it, but never knowing how to get off the merry-go-round of self-pity.

I dare you to take a closer look at your life. You likely have skills you have been downplaying for years. People with low self-confidence have a habit of "dumbing themselves down" in an attempt to downplay their skills, talents, and gifts while at the same time extolling those of others.

False humility (which is really pride in disguise) is another indication of low self-confidence. You will downplay the compliments you receive, even as you freely lavish them on others.

Until you grow up enough to change the way you see yourself, you will always see others as being more, having more, enjoying life more, and deserving more than you. Stop believing this self-deception.

Instead of doing what it takes to change your situation, you will grow increasingly bitter and angry and you will go to your grave a bitter, old man, or woman, still disgruntled over the bad hand you felt you were dealt in life, never stopping to realize you had a good hand, you just never bothered playing it.

Five quick and easy ways to knock envy from your mind and boost your self-confidence:

Look good — if you haven't shopped for new clothes since Y2K, it's time to go shopping. Our esteem and confidence depends heavily upon our appearance. If we feel good about ourselves, it shows inside and out. Looking better on the outside makes us feel better on the inside. When we feel better on the inside, it shows in our walk, our talk and even how we hold our head. You will begin to walk with your head up, not always walking as if you are searching for pennies on the ground. Get your head up; self-confident people always walk with their head up, never down. Practice it until it becomes part of you.

Find something you're good at — People with high self-confidence are masters of their trade. Mastery takes focus, hard work, commitment, and practice. They have committed their whole selves to learning and practicing their craft, whatever it may be. You have been given by God special gifts and talents; and, what a waste it is fretting over people who are making the most of theirs while you allow yours to dry up and die.

Don't hate people because they are making the most of every opportunity — get out there and do the same.

Do something positive — Life is meant to be enjoyed. One of the most enjoyable experiences is doing something for someone who can do absolutely nothing for you in return. Find someone to be kind to everyday, if nothing more than holding open a door or saying a kind word. If you want to be blessed, try being a blessing every once in a while. You will be surprised at what comes back. We reap what we sow, and that means good stuff.

Treat yourself — get a manicure, a facial, a pedicure, or a massage. Allow yourself the luxury of being pampered. Set a little money aside each pay period until you have saved up enough for a real treat. You deserve it and it will make you feel good having rewarded yourself for your hard work. Don't wait for someone else to pamper you, pamper yourself.

Get up and get moving! — This one is especially important. Stop sitting around feeling sorry for yourself. Develop a workout routine that works for you. Workouts are personal, so don't try to adopt someone else's. What works for them may not work for you. Health clubs have staff more than willing to help you find a program that fits you. You can't feel good and look good if your body isn't in good shape. Exercising also causes the body to release endorphins, proteins in the brain that produce a natural high that makes you feel great after a good workout. Looking good and feeling good will boost your self-confidence every time.

FEAR

"God did not give us the spirit of fear" (2 Tim. 1:7). Therefore, if fear didn't originate from God, guess from whom it did? Fear will stop us dead in our tracks and not only prevent us from reaching emotional maturity, but will also prevent us from reaching our fullest potential and realizing our purpose.

When fear enters, confidence exits. The size of our self-confidence is limited by the size of our fear. The more self-confidence we have, the lesser the degree of our fear. The same is true in reverse. The more fearful we are, the less self-confidence we will have. The presence of fear means the absolute absence of courage. It is impossible to be courageous and fearful at the same time. If we lack courage, we will forever languish in the background of life as permanent wallflowers, having wilted and died before ever finding the courage to blossom into the person we were created to be.

What are we so afraid of? Who are you afraid of? The number one thing that people fear (excluding the phobia-type fears), are other people. We are afraid of what people may say or think about us. We fall into this mode of pleasing people when we are children. We learn from the crib to the grave to be people pleasers. It begins with pleasing mom and dad, then the teachers at school, then the professors in college, next, our future spouse, and then our boss and colleagues, then our children, then our friends, then our grandkids, then our great-grandkids...and then, we die.

We rarely manage to get around to pleasing ourselves. To be honest, some of us have never taken the time to get to know ourselves well enough to know what exactly it is we want.

While we spend so much time concerned about what other people may say or think, they could care less if we are doing the same.

For some of us, our self-confidence is eroded when we think for one moment that someone has his or her nose out of joint because of something we have said or done to offend them. We never learned how to stand on our own two feet. As a result, we will go overboard by trying to win back so-called friends instead of spending that time building up the confidence we need to break away from their menacing hold. We will never reach emotional maturity until we cut loose the puppet strings held tightly by others.

Another deterrent to us reaching full maturity is doubt. We doubt our own abilities and capabilities while downplaying any notion that we could be wrong. We will defer to others while playing ourselves small and cheap. Doubt is the enemy of faith. So diametrically opposed is doubt and faith that they cannot even exist together in the same room, let alone in the same body. Emotionally mature people are not afraid to step out into the deep because they have faith enough to believe they will not drown. Emotional maturity begins when we start to act as if our faith is greater than our doubts, our courage greater than our fears and our confidence greater than our self-pity.

BALANCE

One of the keystone elements of emotional maturity that is frequently overlooked is balance. In a time of 24/7 news cycles, the Internet, Blackberry and iPhone we have become terribly unbalanced. The line between work and home has been obliterated because there is never a time that we are not connected to work. Our stress levels, blood pressure levels, and cholesterol levels are steadily moving north while our quality of life is steadily sliding south. The once three-legged stool of work, home, and church has now morphed into some monstrous hybrid of almost unidentifiable and unmanageable proportions as we struggle to keep everything working together.

Many of us have reached a critical tipping point and are just waiting for the stool to completely collapse. However, before the stool completely collapses, let's explore ways to pull our lives back to the center, back into balance, and given the state of the economy, do it all on the cheap:

Plan — the most stressful times are unplanned times. To the degree that you can plan your week, sit down on Sunday with the kids if they are still home and synchronize calendars so that there won't be any surprises during the week. Plan in down time, if it is nothing more than taking the shoes off after work and sitting quietly on the couch for 15 minutes before beginning the evening. You would be surprised at the difference that 15 minutes can make. Planning is key to balance.

Work hard, play harder — never sacrifice vacation time, paid time off, or any of the time you have worked hard to accumulate. Never give time back, you've worked hard for it. They're not "giving" you anything, it is your time. Make time to play. Somewhere along the way, we have forgotten how to laugh, play, and have fun. Go toss a Frisbee, fly a kite in the park, or go on a leisurely bike ride. Fun doesn't have to be elaborate or expensive.

Get organized — scattered things means a scattered life. Things scattered around the house or around the office tend to make us scatterbrained and stressed. Get rid of stuff you no longer need. Clean up and clear out the clutter.

Begin the day in quiet meditation — this sets the pace for the entire day. If you begin the day rushed, you will be rushed all day. For me, this means spending time alone with God, committing my day to Him, and seeking His guidance and wisdom on the decisions I have to make, the meetings I have to attend, and the people with whom I am meeting that day. For you, that could mean something totally different. But life is too complicated to try to figure out on our own.

Leave work at work — No one's indispensable. If you dropped dead on Monday, your job will likely be filled by Friday. Do an excellent job, but leave the job at the job.

Emotional maturity is not easy. In fact, it is one, long, sometimes very lonely, painful road to tread. You can't find it in a book, and you can earn ten doctorate degrees and still be emotionally immature.

Nothing can prepare us for life but life. Maturity comes through the twists, turns, trials, failures, setbacks, betrayals, and adversities of everyday life. If you're not there yet, be patient with yourself. If you have failed, even failed miserably, as I so many times have — get back up and try again. Pick up the pieces and live again. All of us will invariably fall, but you're not a failure when you fall. You're a failure when you quit.

~~~~~~

I believe we have two lives, the life we learn with
and the life we live with after that.

- Glenn Close as Iris Gaines
from the movie, "The Natural"
(Sony Pictures 1984)

~~~~~~

The most important person to get to know

is you — you're with you wherever you go.

Know where you're strong, but most of all weak

because that is the area the enemy will seek.

Don't ever say what you won't do.

Life has a way of surprising you.

But you have the power, you get to decide

if your life will be nothing or one heck of a ride!

Conclusion:
Sabotage or Success? It's your choice.

*"I call heaven and earth to witness against you today, that
I have set before you life and death, the blessing and the
curse. So choose life in order that you may live, you and your
descendants."*

Deuteronomy 30:19

Thank you for allowing me to share my thoughts with
you. You could have spent your time reading far greater
literary works, but you chose to spend your time with me and
for that, I thank you. This is my first book and I didn't know
quite what to expect. I was given what to me was an almost
impossible assignment. Without the guidance of my Lord and
Savior Jesus Christ, there is no way I could have done it. To
Him, I am grateful.

It is my hope that the things we have learned together
will serve you well on your life's journey. Our path is never
straight and rarely without pitfalls along the way. This book is a

culmination of tests and trials, adversities and failures, but the good news is that I found my way back and so can you.

Even though it was entirely unintentional, the chapters are deliberately laid out in such a way as to serve as a code and as a reminder to us all that life is complicated. There are certain laws of the universe and of God that none of us can break or can afford to ignore without penalty. And the penalty will likely consist of failure and loss in some measurable degree.

I have offered these truths as they were revealed to me and if you look more closely I believe you will be astounded at how seven seemingly disjointed reasons can coalesce to bring about one life changing result.

F orfeiting Our Purpose
A rrogance
I gnoring the Core
L ying
U nderestimating Risks
R uling out the Rules
E motional Immaturity

Seven reasons, one astounding result. The capacity to fall prey to any one or all of these is great. As fallible people living in a fallen world they lie dormant inside us all — waiting for the right opportunity, the right circumstance, the right person or thing under the right conditions to take away our focus and lead us down dangerous paths.

Apart from a relationship with Jesus Christ, they will capture us and convince us that we are right and everyone else is wrong, including God. I am not so naïve to believe that there are only seven reasons why human beings fall. However, I do trust the word of God enough to believe that directly or indirectly one or more of these seven, or a facet of them, will be the wrecking ball that will demolish overnight what took years to build.

Your life and my life is a culmination of our choices. The quality of life you are enjoying today or the lack of quality you are suffering through today is largely due to the choices you made yesterday — some good, others not so good. Yet, you still have the power to choose. Choose wisely. Otherwise, any one of these seven alone or together will ruin your relationships, short circuit your career, or destroy your life.

Sabotage or success? It's your choice.

The grass withers, the
flower fades,
But the word of our God
stands forever.
(Isaiah 40:8)

ENDNOTES

Chapter 1

1.Taken from various sources, including:
http://rootzoo.com/articles/view/NCAA-Football/General/
Remembering-Roy- Wrong-Way-Riegels
http://sportsillustrated.cnn.com/vault/article/magazine/
MAG1129184/index.htm

2.Taken from various sources, including: Http://dictionary.reference.com/browse/Devour.

3. ©2007 Dr. Alan R. Zimmerman. Reprinted with permission from Dr. Alan Zimmerman's Internet newsletter, the 'Tuesday Tip.' For your own personal, free subscription to the 'Tuesday Tip' as well as information on Dr. Zimmerman's keynotes and seminars, go to http://www.drzimmerman.com/ or call 800-621-7881.

Chapter 2

1. As adapted from Ovid, *Metamorphoses,* Book 3.

2. Matt Apuzzo, *Abramoff Gets Four Years for Corruption,* The Associated Press, The Dallas Morning News, September 5, 2008.

Chapter 3

1. Jiminy Cricket from the film Pinocchio. Walt Disney films, 1940.

Chapter 4

1. *The Story of the King and the Four Girls* used by permission from D.L. Ashliman. Charles Swynnerton, *Indian Nights' Entertainment;* or, *Folk-Tales from the Upper Indus,* ed. D.L. Ashliman. (London: Elliott Stock, 1892, no. 22), 56-62.

2. Nelson's *New Illustrated Bible Dictionary*, ed. Ronald F. Young-blood, F.F. Bruce and R.K. Harrison (Nashville, TN: Thomas Nelson Publishers, 1995), 767.

Chapter 6

1. Taken from various sources, including: http://en.wikipedia.org/wiki/The_Dog_and_its_Reflection.

Chapter 7

1. from the story, "Nails in the Fence," Author Unknown - http://www.inspirationpeak.com/cgi-bin/stories.cgi?record=50

About the Author

Dorothy Burton is a native Texan and a former four-term City Council member for the City of Duncanville, Texas, a suburb of Dallas. The first African-American elected to the Council, she served as the city's first At-Large representative and was twice elected Mayor Pro Tem. Dorothy is a conference speaker and workshop leader for various public sector and faith-based organizations across the country. In 2013 she founded Christians in Public Service, Inc., a 501 (c)(3) non-profit, non-denominational, non-partisan organization with a mission to encourage and equip Christian public servants to serve, lead, and govern from a biblical frame of reference. www.christiansinpublicservice.org.

Dorothy has been actively involved for over two decades in public service. With a passion for servant leadership, she served on the National League of Cities Women in Municipal Government Board of Directors and is a graduate of the University of Texas at Arlington, earning a Bachelor of Arts in Journalism and a Master of Arts in Urban Affairs. Dorothy is a graduate of Dallas Theological Seminary, earning a Master of Arts in Christian Leadership and a Graduate Teacher Diploma from the Evangelical Training Association. She is a charter graduate of Dallas Blueprint for Leadership, a graduate of Leadership Southwest and the prestigious Leadership Texas.

Dorothy has been married for over 30 years to Dr. Michael Burton. They are the parents of one grown daughter, Jessica, and reside in the Dallas area.

www.christiansinpublicservice.org
dorothy@dorothyburton.com

To the Fallen Believer

Life is not dress rehearsal my friend,
we don't get to do this all over again.
God still has something He wants you to do.
Get back in the game. He still loves you.
Okay, you've messed up and have never been this down.
But dust yourself off and take a quick look around.
No one is perfect. We all have our faults.
So away with self-pity and negative thoughts!

God who began a good work in you
is able to complete it, if you'll allow Him to.
Suffering is temporary and pain has its place,
but neither of these is greater than His grace.

Our life is like a vapor, it too will dissipate.
But as long as we *have* life it's never too late.
Dream new dreams. Set challenging new goals.
Begin today, before the bell tolls.

Don't be like those facing death that say,
"If only I had another week, another day."
John Whittier said it best, before taking his rest —
"For all sad words of tongue and pen,
the saddest are these, it might have been."

Do what you can, do it while you can,
even your failure was part of His plan.
Your life's not over because you've taken a fall.
It's just life, and life happens to us all.

Get up, get moving, it's a brand new day.
Don't worry about what people will say.
Care not what people think. Your life is God's call.
No matter what you've done, Jesus paid for it all.